Witness
to Evil

BERGEN-BELSEN

1945

Isaac Levy

PETER HALBAN
in association with
THE EUROPEAN JEWISH PUBLICATION SOCIETY

To my dear wife, Tonie,
who so stoically shared the burden
of my anxieties and frustrations

FIRST PUBLISHED IN GREAT BRITAIN BY
PETER HALBAN PUBLISHERS LTD
42 South Molton Street
London W1Y 1HB
1995

British Library Cataloguing-in-Publication Data.

A catalogue record for this book is available from the British Library.

ISBN 1 870015 58 4

The poem *Shema* by Primo Levi is reproduced with kind
permission of Faber and Faber Ltd and Ruth Feldman and
Brian Swann, the translators.

Phototypeset by Computape (Pickering) Ltd, North Yorkshire
Printed and bound in Great Britain by
The Lavenham Press, Lavenham, Suffolk

CONTENTS

GLOSSARY

Aliyah	Immigration to Israel
Am Yisrael Chai	'The People of Israel Lives' (generally used in popular song
Brit Milah	Circumcision
Galut	Diaspora (lit. exile)
Gemeinde	Community
Judenschmerz	Jewish pain
Kaddish	Prayer for the dead
Li'chvod Ha'Oreach	In honour of our guest
Magen David	Star of David
Mikvah	Ritual bath
Mischling	Mixed race – Jewish and non-Jewish
Mitzvah	Good deed
Olim	Immigrant or pilgrim to Israel (lit. going up)
Oneg Shabbat	A pleasant Sabbath gathering
Pesach	Passover
Schechitah	Ritual slaughter
She'erit Ha'Pletah	The surviving few
Seder	Passover feast
Sifrei Torah	Scrolls of the Law (Pentateuch)
So Schactet der Jude	'Thus does the Jew slaughter'
Szid	Polish for Jew (abusive)
Yamim Noraim	Days of awe (around Jewish New Year ending on the Day of Atonement)

FOREWORD

My personal memoir of the period 1941–4 appeared in 1978 under the title *Now I Can Tell: Middle East Memories*. Since then I have been urged by friends and associates who read that book to write a sequel covering the years 1944–5 when I served as Senior Jewish Chaplain to the British Liberation Army and experienced the trauma following the liberation of the Belsen concentration camp and its concomitant political, social and religious complications.

I persistently refused to do so – not because of indolence but from a sense of impotence to offer a purely factual presentation unaffected by the disturbing emotions which memories evoke. This combined with a reluctance to record my involvement in frequent controversy with the authorities.

When I participated in the historic First International Conference of Children of Holocaust Survivors held in New York in May 1984, and delivered an address on Belsen in the presence of more than 1700 young people, memories of those horrendous years were painfully revived. This occasion offered me the opportunity for a reunion with a number of Belsen survivors with whom I had worked closely. They too tried to persuade me to record my experiences saying that I was duty bound to do so. I still felt unable to comply with their wishes.

What then prompted me, after the passage of so many years,

to put pen to paper? Strange as it may seem, the catalyst was Menachem, the son of Yossel and Hadassah Rosensaft. Menachem was born in Belsen. He has written the most moving poetry, and is now a successful international lawyer. He was the founder and first chairman of the International Network of Children of Jewish Holocaust Survivors. On a visit to London, he came to see me and his presence revived memories of his parents who had been responsible for the creation of the Central Jewish Committee in Belsen, and their struggles to obtain due consideration for the special needs of Jewish inmates of the camps.

He presented cogent arguments that my testimony as an eye-witness was essential because, with the passing years, there would be a paucity of reliable witnesses to that painful chapter of Jewish history. I therefore agreed. I proceeded to read the hundreds of letters I had written to my wife who so diligently preserved them and to whom I poured out all my bitter frustrations, and without disclosing military secrets wrote a daily account of my painful experiences. I re-examined documents and memoranda, now yellowing with age. I reread correspondence which passed between me and various organisations which were supposed to help us deal with the problems which seemed to accumulate almost daily. All this previously un-published material helped me to revive faded memories and to relive the experiences of that distant past.

The notorious Belsen concentration camp was liberated by the British Army on 15 April 1945 and the citizens of the United Kingdom were made fully aware for the first time that such a death factory actually existed. Until then the only camps which received any mention were Dachau and Buchenwald and vague rumours circulated about a place called Auschwitz. It took all too long for the full implications of Hitler's Final Solution to make an impact.

There was a strange and inexplicable reluctance to admit to such horrors and callous inhumanity. Jewish refugees from Germany and central Europe had been permitted to arrive in England in the early 1930s on condition that they were supported by friends or Jewish organisations and would not become a burden on the state. At the outbreak of war, many hundreds of them enlisted in the army albeit at first only to serve in the Pioneer Corps as members of a non-combatant labour force. These men had a tale to tell about the treatment meted out to them at the hands of the Nazis, but reports of atrocities were suppressed prior to Britain's declaration of war.

Only when it suited the war propaganda machine were efforts made to circulate the truth. The full implications of what concentration camps were designed to achieve were all too vaguely described or understood. Bad news travels fast but not when it is inadequately expressed, or when for political reasons it is hushed up. Hitler's rise to power was deemed Germany's internal affair. His treatment of Jews may have been verbally condemned by the passing of pious resolutions, but evinced no positive action on the part of the free nations of the West. *Kristallnacht*, 9–10 November 1938, was a clear indication of what was in store for continental Jewry, but was not seen as a pointer to the horrors yet to come. Appeasement, the dominant theme at the time, could only be interpreted by some of us as an apathetic attitude to the fate of European Jewry.

The fact that Oswald Mosley and his British Union of Fascists were permitted to parade through the streets of London in their uniforms, glorying in their Hitler salutes, was profoundly disturbing. Those of us who were active in the anti-Fascist movement used every opportunity to denounce Mosley and his henchmen, proclaiming that they and their doctrine were not just anti-Semitic but that they also spelt a threat to democracy and should therefore be denied the freedom of

speech which they enjoyed. We were equally disturbed by the
apparent indifference displayed by the Board of Deputies, the
official representative organisation of British Jewry, to the
Fascist threat in that they were reluctant to adopt an openly
anti-Fascist stance, preferring to restrict themselves to a defen-
sive attitude to any anti-Jewish statement emanating from the
B.U.F.

The outbreak of war changed all this. The menace of
Hitlerism was acknowledged, its satellite Fascists were interned
for the duration of the war and Britain at last resolved to adopt
the necessary measures to combat the threat which Germany's
advancing armies presented to the peace of the world.

The dire effects of Hitler's wartime occupation of Europe
became known to those of us who served with the British
Liberation Army. We can testify from personal experience and
from the impact which everything we witnessed had on us.

1995 will mark the fiftieth anniversary of the end of World
War II and the liberation of Belsen. I can only hope that my
memoir of 1945 will serve as a contribution to the observance
of that historic event.

Isaac Levy
London, 1994

SHEMA

You who live secure
In your warm houses,
Who, returning at evening, find
Hot food and friendly faces:
    Consider whether this is a man,
    Who labours in the mud
    Who knows no peace
    Who fights for a crust of bread
    Who dies at a yes or a no.
    Consider whether this is a woman
    Without hair or name
    With no more strength to remember
    Eyes empty and womb cold
    As a frog in winter.
Consider that this has been:
I commend these words to you.
Engrave them on your hearts
When you are in your house, when you walk on your way
When you go to bed, when you rise:
repeat them to your children.

Primo Levi
10 January 1946

1

AFTER SERVING FOR three years in the Middle East I was posted to Europe to assume the office of Senior Jewish Chaplain to the British Liberation Army, later to be called the British Army of the Rhine.

At the time of my arrival the Army had established its Headquarters in Brussels and on reporting for duty there I was informed that I was to be attached to the 2nd Army which was then rapidly advancing into Holland. During my all too brief stay in Brussels I had the opportunity to gain my first insight into the malevolence of the Nazi occupation. A rather vague report reached me of a prison in the town of Malines in which Jews had been incarcerated by the Nazis.

What I saw on entering this empty building immediately conveyed a painful reality. I went from cell to cell and saw carved on the walls a variety of messages, prayers and cries of desperation from the hapless victims. The Magen David which appeared so frequently was indisputable evidence of the identity of the former inmates. The ultimate fate of these Jews was not known at the time. Only later did it transpire that this prison was used as a transit stage for transportation to the death camps of Eastern Europe.

I travelled to Holland and there I received further confirmation of malicious Nazi activity. As I was passing through Vught in south Holland I saw a large enclosed area which appeared to be completely deserted. It had obviously been some sort of camp – there were a variety of huts. The place was clinically clean, as though it had never been occupied, and over all there was a strange eeriness. I walked around not seeing a soul until, as I was about to leave, a sad looking man appeared who, I realised, must be a caretaker or something of the sort. We had difficulty in communicating since he had no English and I had no Dutch. I reluctantly used a few words of German knowing that this was not a popular language in a country which had suffered German occupation. He did, however, convey to me that this had been a concentration camp and that three crematoria had operated here, one of which was smaller than the other two. This had been the children's crematorium, small in size to save fuel. As though this information was not sickening enough, as I was about to leave the place I noticed a piece of paper lying on the ground. I picked it up and to my horror saw that it was the label of a Zyklon B gas canister which was further, ample proof that this had once been a concentration camp.

The whole area was so completely cleansed of any trace of maltreatment that I could only presume that the Dutch, who were full of hatred for the Germans, had cleared up the camp to erase any trace of its previous function. That label left a profound impression on me. I kept it as a confirmation of the reports then current of the horrendous extermination methods used by the Nazis.

As I continued my journey through Holland with the advancing army, I became increasingly obsessed with the desire to ascertain the fate of any Jews who may have survived German occupation, convinced as I was that I would ultimately meet them and learn from them how they had succeeded in eluding the fate to which Jews had been exposed.

To my intense delight such an opportunity was afforded to me as I passed through Enschede, a town on the Dutch–German border. It was here that I was privileged to meet a young Dutch Rabbi and his wife who, thanks to the kindness of a local doctor, had remained in hiding within a short distance of their synagogue during the whole period of the occupation. Their house adjoined the synagogue and, thanks to the few tins of Kosher food which I had in my possession, I could provide them with a kosher meal — their first in many years. This delightful couple gave me an insight into the privations which Dutch Jewry had suffered under the Nazis.

Enschede was once a prosperous community and the town had been the centre of the textile industry. The synagogue, built 15 years previously, was a ghastly sight. All the furniture and fittings had been removed and the place had been used as a storehouse for potatoes and for furniture taken from the homes of deported Jews. The worst sight was the cellar which had been reconstructed to contain nine cells in which 40–50 prisoners could be incarcerated.

Now that the Rabbi and his wife could breathe freely again, their major concern was for the future of children whose parents, before their deportation, had deposited them with Christian families. Their fully justified fear was that those children whose lives had been saved, at great risk on the part of their rescuers, would be lost to the community. There was every reason to suspect that they might have been baptised by their foster parents and in time would have no recollection of their Jewish origins. The Rabbi rightly felt that the situation was desperate. Were he to publicise the problem, it might re-awaken dormant anti-Semitism. Even though the Dutch population was on the whole sympathetic to the plight of Jewry, the religious issue was so sensitive that it had to be treated with great delicacy and perspicacity.

As the Rabbi succinctly put it — the Nazis wished to destroy our bodies, but the kindness of the Dutch may destroy our souls. We were later to learn that this was not a problem unique to Holland, but applied equally to other countries where Jewish children had been entrusted to the care of sympathetic Christian families and with the passing of time had been reared as practising Christians.

I left them with a heavy heart realising what an uphill struggle faced them in their efforts to rebuild a shattered community with such limited resources.

2

TO ENTER GERMANY with a conquering army was an exhilarating experience in itself, but to do so during Pesach week added to its significance. I held the Sedarim on the outskirts of Goch, between the river Maas and the Rhine. Thanks to the facilities provided by the army, some 200 men attended. It was my good fortune to enjoy the friendship of Brigadier George Allen who was in charge of Corps administration – my wife and I had been billeted with his sister back in England. His cooperation greatly eased any problem I might have had in making Pesach arrangements.

We first met in the Middle East when, as a Lieutenant-Colonel, he was in command of a Tank Regiment. He struck me then as a lively, ebullient person ready to be helpful. As far as I was concerned he was particularly cooperative in that he made facilities available for the Jewish personnel under his command. When, on this occasion, we renewed our assocation, he had advanced in rank and, as I later ascertained, he was one of General Montgomery's 'blue-eyed boys'. To my great sorrow, I was to learn from his sister shortly after the war that he had been killed in a road accident.

I approached him and explained that I was planning Pesach celebrations. Without a moment's hesitation he placed his catering officer at my disposal who, with great enthusiasm, comandeered crockery and cutlery from the local inhabitants and ensured that all the supplies which I provided were tastefully presented. The atmosphere was electric. We all knew that before many more days had passed we would be advancing deep into German territory. We all felt elated for this was an historic Pesach, the like of which we would never experience again. We were re-enacting an Exodus to freedom. We were on the eve of victory. The enemy would soon be vanquished and the Nazi tyranny would be at an end. We sang the Seder songs lustily, wished each other a happy Yom Tov and dispersed. I bade the men farewell for on the morrow I would cross the Rhine to enter the domain of the greatest evil of modern times.

The euphoria of the moment left me and was replaced by the memories of Malines, Vught and Enschede, but little did I realise that those earlier impressions were only a foretaste of what was to come. I was soon to be confronted by the most devastating of my wartime experiences.

The army was advancing rapidly into Westphalia, but the final objective had yet to be met. News reached us that somewhere in the vicinity of Hanover the forward troops had reached a locality where a truce had been negotiated with the local German military Commander because of an outbreak of typhus. It all sounded rather vague and the details released conveyed little.

I hurried to the area and learned that the news which had reached us referred to a concentration camp called Belsen near the village of Bergen. But it appeared that there was no truth in the report that typhus raged there. What I discovered was a former *Wehrmacht* barracks. The sight which greeted me as I entered this enclosure was unbelievable. Crowds of men and women were milling around, some dressed in tattered clothing others in striped pyjamas of a sort.

I had expected to find broken bodies, emaciated human beings, tortured souls – at least that was how my imagination pictured any inmates of concentration camps. How could the Nazi doctrine permit Jews to appear like normal human beings? But the people I saw looked fairly healthy. They were jubilant, excited and exultant; they crowded round me and shouted Shalom. I was overwhelmed. I was the first British officer whom they had seen who actually wore a Magen David on his cap; a Jewish officer who, to their delight, belonged to a liberating army. Then to my astonishment they insisted that I stand on an improvised platform and address them in the best Yiddish that I could muster. But words failed me. I was overcome with emotion especially when I saw that so many of them wore a cardboard home-made badge on which was drawn a blue and white Magen David. This was their assertion that the Jewish people lived and in spite of the cruel privations which had been suffered was indestructible. The Nazis had forced them to wear a yellow star on their clothing but now that star assumed a new shape and meaning.

The gathering gave the impression of being well organised, prepared for any eventuality, and not a leaderless group of individuals. The inmates of these barracks were indeed served by a leader, a dynamic man of small stature but of a fiery disposition who, on seeing me enter the camp, took control and organised a welcoming demonstration. He it was who acted as spokesman conveying to me the joy which his fellow inmates felt at their long awaited liberation. He introduced himself as Yossel Rosensaft. All I could do was to asssure him that I shared with him and all his comrades the exhilaration of this momentous occasion.

So this was the camp which bore the name of Bergen-Belsen – not too bad, I thought. These people had survived and looked in fairly good shape in spite of the ordeals they must have undergone. But I was soon to be disillusioned for Yossel informed me that this was only a section of the whole camp, the better part; much worse was that which existed a short distance away. I promised to keep in contact with him and left the barracks, which later became known as the upper camp. A short drive brought me to a large area enclosed by wire at the entrance of which British soldiers stood on guard preventing unauthorised admission. That earlier report had been correct. Typhus raged in the camp. Those who were permitted entry were subjected to a dusting of DDT. Up their sleeves, down their trousers, into their shirts or uniforms, the necessary protection against lice which were the carriers of this deadly infection.

Armed with this immunity I walked into the hell of Belsen, there to see the full extent of the vicious treatment meted out to the tens of thousands of hapless victims of Nazi ferocity. Heaps of corpses were lying in the main pathways. Those who still had a little life in them were crawling on all fours in search of scraps of food. Haggard, starved bodies, bulging eyes, pitifully appealing for help.

I entered some of the huts which accommodated hundreds of emaciated bodies lying in the tiered bunks. The nauseating smell was unbearable. These wretched victims were lying in indescribable filth. At first sight it was impossible to distinguish between the barely living and the dead, for those who still had the barest trace of life looked lifeless. The raging typhus, starvation, lack of sanitation, no running water and the spread of dysentery had taken an appalling toll. Hundreds died every day and little or no effort had been made to remove the corpses.

To enter these huts was like a descent into Dante's *Inferno*. I tried to talk to some of the inmates offering a word of encouragement and hope, but as I tried to communicate with one man who seemed a little articulate, he breathed his last. The sense of helplessness was overwhelming. These poor people needed food and medical attention not words of encouragement. What did I have to offer?

By the time I arrived at this camp, three days after the first

British soldiers had entered the camp, some effort had been made to provide medical aid. A Casualty Clearing Station, a Light Field Ambulance and a Field Hygiene Section were installed. One of the first medical teams was commanded by Captain J. Ellis Stone, who after the war beame a close friend and our family doctor.★ The appalling condition of the camp was beyond the capacity of these army medical units. There was a desperate shortage of doctors, nurses, drugs and essentials for adequate treatment. The absence of a common language between the doctors and their patients was an added hindrance. The estimated number of inmates was 50,000 of whom 20,000 suffered from the most virulent of diseases requiring urgent hospitalisation, and many thousands would die if they were not removed and given the appropriate food.

The psychological effect on these young doctors was devastating. I well recall a conversation I had with members of the C.C.S. one evening. They were relaxing after a long and gruelling day and were drinking heavily, sinking into a state of complete intoxication. 'If we were not to drink,' they said, 'we would go stark staring mad. We are doctors and are supposed to heal, but this task is hopeless. They die on us as soon as we touch them.'

Within the first two or three weeks after liberation, no less than 20,000 corpses were removed from the huts and from the heaps lying in the main paths. This task was allotted to the Hungarian and S.S. guards, male and female, who had been detained in the camp after the surrender. Owing to the vast numbers involved, the most expedient method of burial was to commit them to mass graves which were prepared by bulldozers provided by the Royal Engineers. The indignity of these burials was deeply disturbing. At first the bodies were dragged by their skeletal legs and cast into the pits. When this proved too slow a process, the bulldozers were employed to shovel

★ He ended his career as Lord Stone. After the War he was raised to the peerage in recognition of his services to Prime Minister Harold Wilson, and to members of his Cabinet .

them in. Despite this crude and horrendous method of disposal of human beings, a short burial service was conducted and the Kaddish recited. This privilege was assigned to me and to my colleague Leslie Hardman who had arrived at Belsen a few days before me.

Both of us were profoundly affected by this most inadequate form of religious ministration. To recite the Kaddish over such a heap of emaciated bodies cast helter-skelter into pits, each containing some 5000 such corpses, seemed to negate the concept of man created in the divine image. Their humanity had been denied them by the Nazis, and now their place of disposal set the seal on that denial. They had not been buried as we would understand the meaning of burial, they were cast into pits without any personal identification, an anonymous mass of skeletons whose flesh had been destroyed by disease and the privations of hunger.

Leslie Hardman had preceded me at Belsen and I must pay tribute to the work he did during those early hectic and heartbreaking days. He placed himself entirely at the disposal of the military authorities and helped to introduce some order into the chaos then prevailing. The sight he witnessed on entering the camp profoundly affected him. When I first saw him he was walking round armed with a pistol. This was highly irregular for we chaplains, by our very calling, were non-combatants and prohibited from carrying weapons. He made some reference to self protection in case he met with resistance which, in my view, was highly unlikely and I had to instruct him to dispose of the pistol which he did. Except for this lapse, he did splendid work, making himself indispensable to the medical and military staff.

On 22 April, I wrote to my wife:

Darling,
I have just returned from my first visit to the death camp of
Belsen, of which you may have read in the press. It was a long
drive and fortunately managed to scrounge a lift with my R.C.

colleague who also went there. It is the 'show place' of the
army and the number of spectators is growing. They probably
go to see what such a place looks like. I, who have seen two
others which had been emptied of their victims, went to find
Jews. And, God, did I find them. And how I found them and
what specimens of humanity they are after the treatment they
have received. I am certain that 90 per cent of those who
survive will never be really normal. They have suffered too
much . . .

I passed through the normal procedure and went to Camp
No. 1, first of all to look for Hardman who has been living
there since last Tuesday or Wednesday. The Colonel and others
had asked me to find him and remove him as he was becoming
hysterical. I walked through the main path which divides the
camp into two, one half for men and the other half for women
and the stench was appalling. I cannot describe the sight of these
walking skeletons. Some are lying down under the projection
between roof and walls of the huts to gain shelter from the
wind and rain, others are just strolling around, their rags barely
covering them. A few young girls are here, too, at least I saw a
few walking around, some are better and healthier in their
appearance than others. I walked on towards the end of the
main pathway. I did not know until afterwards that I was
walking in the direction of the mass cemetery where thousands
are being buried in a common grave. Yes, my darling,
thousands. When the camp was taken there were no less than
36,000 dead awaiting burial. Can you visualise it? And the
present number of inmates is in the region of 56,000. The
majority of the women are Jewish. By chance I overheard a
conversation in Yiddish. I stopped and spoke to the women and
introduced myself. Immediately I was overwhelmed with their
story. Taken from Poland to one camp, and passed on to
another, each one better than the former. Better food and
housing but made to work like slaves. Hair short at first began
to grow again but after many fluctuations they were brought
here to die of starvation. Yes, the Nazis did not touch them,
they just did not feed them and they developed diseases and the
emaciated bodies fell victim to typhus, dysentery, tuberculosis
etc. And they died in their thousands. It was whilst I was talking

to these women that I saw two young girls wearing a yellow star on their backs. I approached them and naturally discovered that they were Jewish. The traces of their former pleasant features are still visible. They came from good families in Prague. Thank God they arrived only a few days before the army liberated them. They are still normal and human. Whilst with them others joined us and soon I had a small gathering around me. It was then that Hardman appeared. I stretched out my hand to greet him and he fell on my neck and wept like a babe. The people round me saw it and joined in the weeping and I had to take him aside and make him pull himself together. He is not hysterical, he is tired and should go away for a while but he refuses to move. He feels that he must stay and bring a word of comfort to these people. He talks of the horrors that they have suffered and I can see that each word is spelt in blood.

He is doing yeoman service there but I fear that it may ruin his health but he refuses to listen to me. He told me as much as he could in the limited time I had. Unfortunately I had to return to Base after being there 2½ hours. But I am going back tomorrow and shall spend two days there with Hardman and together we shall try and do something to help these people. And to talk to the authorities. Already I have laid the foundation of a plan but we cannot carry it out since it must come from above.

I have interrupted this letter to go across to the medical people here. The hour is late since I have been with them for over an hour. I have at least achieved this that I have obtained from them a complete picture of the medical problem and an insight into their attitude. They are ready to help in every way and I have asked the Brigadier's assistance in the absence of his chief to write to the authorities asking for the special appointment of chaplains and Relief Groups for the task. The horror Camp I am told contains 34,000 people still and there are 1,500 cases of typhus to deal with besides the other diseases. It is an appalling task but every effort is being made to cope with it. I have the backing of the authorities and we shall now get to work . . .

26 April '45

Tonie dearest,

I am sorry to say that for the last few days you have had to take a secondary place in my thoughts and time. I just could not write. For four days I have been in the Concentration Camp and twice I tried to write to you, enclosed are the results. I just couldn't. I was utterly exhausted by the end of the day. It has been a most gruelling time. I had to return to Base today because we are moving again or else I would have stayed there.

I just cannot leave Hardman alone. He is working like a maniac down there. And on my return here I had a wash and sit down to write to the press. I am enclosing a copy for you. It is not literary. I wrote just as the spirit moved me. Perhaps it is not good enough but I cannot help it. One just cannot write about this place in words. I have helped to organise some of the work. Hardman is running around and is lost in the multifarious tasks. I had to lend a hand and try and get things going. Thank God we have managed to achieve something but it is far from adequate.

We need help so badly. Are there any Relief Groups, if so where are they and when will they come? We need men and women who are capable of putting up with the worst possible conditions and who can stand up to the strain and exposure to typhus and disease. I have lived amongst it now for these four days and realise what is required – a cast-iron constitution and a desire to help and a knowledge of Yiddish and German. It is beyond all comprehension and description. The death rate is appalling and the sight of corpses no longer worries you after a while. It is the living. We have to save lives and God knows how we can do it. Their poor bodies are so emaciated and weak that they will fall at the least provocation even the healthy ones are beginning to crack up.

Now I hear that another camp may soon be unearthed and who will help us then? I just cannot devote all of my time to it since some of the military work must go on. Unless we receive help from England these people will be left without any aid. I am writing to Brodie tonight. I do not know whether he is back. But we must have men. Chaplains can do excellent work and we must have them here. The duty towards the men takes secondary place now. We have thousands of our people to help and they are helpless and wretched.

Read this letter which I have written to the J.C. and tell me whether it is enough. I am racing against time too and would to God that I could find more hours in the day. I am desperately tired and need to sleep but thanks to your coffee I shall dope myself and carry on.

This is the letter that I sent to the *Jewish Chronicle*:

The world is hearing of the death camp of Bergen-Belsen, the notorious concentration camp recently liberated by our forces. The press and the radio will make references to it and the 'sights' which many may come to see. What thought will be given to the tens of thousands of Jewish inmates I wonder. My colleague the Rev. L.H. Hardman, has been here since the second day of liberation and I joined him a few days later. Together we are helping the Military Government to bring some order into an appalling chaos. WE NEED HELP. Are there any Jewish Groups of Relief Workers ready to join us?

I feel I owe it to the Jewish community back home to give them some idea of the sights one sees in this ghastly camp, but there are no words to describe the indescribable, nor can one adequately convey the tragedy and misery of tens of thousands of hapless victims. There are two camps, numbers one and two. Number one is the horror camp. The stench reaches to high heaven. Death stalks abroad. Thousands have died already in these last few days and daily the toll rises. To date we have buried some 20,000 men, women and children, and there are more to follow. The medical authorities are fighting a hopeless battle. Typhus is raging furiously as are T.B. and dysentery.

People are moving round the camp looking like human skeletons. Children are cooped up with their parents and living in the midst of unimaginable squalor. They lie on the filthy floors clothed in rags and tatters. Lice and vermin everywhere. When the liberating forces arrived they found corpses lying around the camp, in the huts and heaped in the main pathways.

The living lay with the dead in close proximity. Corpses were used as pillows and mattresses. In one hut which I visited lay some thirty women all suffering from the diseases rampant in the camp. Three corpses lay there with them and had been there for five days. They begged me to have the corpses removed so that they could at least remain with the living. In another hut were young women still comparatively healthy who refused to leave their sick and dying comrades. They have been moulded into new families and call each other '*Lager Schwester*'!

Mass burials are taking place daily. The corpses are cast into vast pits dug by the army bulldozers. Each of these pits contains at least 5000 corpses. Meanwhile, the death rate is growing. Starvation and disease take their daily toll. Food is now available but these emaciated bodies cannot digest it. They cry out for white bread and a light diet. A young girl pleads with us 'Give me food that I can eat or before long I shall join the heap of corpses.' A daughter approaches us begging us to help her mother who is too weak to contain her food. We are all too well aware that it is a race against time.

My colleague and I are attempting to list the names of survivors. An impossible task for we cannot be certain the record will be accurate. Some die even as we list them. We need help. Will men and women in England volunteer for relief work and join us? Will they arrive in time? Belsen is just the beginning, we may yet find more of our brethren in other camps, if and when we arrive in time. We shall need help then. IS MY CALL IN VAIN OR WILL HELP YET COME?

On that same day in April, I also wrote to Rabbi Brodie, the Senior Jewish Chaplain in London:

I have just returned from a short stay in the recently liberated Belsen concentration camp. I have had to write to the Jewish Chronicle direct about it because of my appeal for relief workers to come out immediately before it is too late. We have been informed that there are several thousands of Jews in these two camps and I need not tell you what our reaction is.

Hardman arrived two days after it was liberated by 8th Corps and has stayed on. He has to do so. We must have chaplains there. A Christian chaplain is there and a Catholic too and Hardman is doing a great job.

The conditions are appalling. Worse than anyone can believe, and I am informed that another camp may shortly be uncovered. If this is true I have to appeal not only for Relief Workers, but for more chaplains for this task. If Christian chaplains can work in these camps and be seconded for this purpose, then in heaven's name we have the right to ask the same. Our claim is greater and more urgent. Both the C. of E.s and the R.C.s have a special increment for these purposes and I appeal to you to press the War Office for two chaplains at least as an 'eclipse increment'. This term has a meaning here and it must register some reaction over there. Hardman and I have to leave everything for this purpose and I am sure that you will agree that we are justified. We cannot think of military duties when this need is so pressing. I fully expect that you will concur.

These are the last relics of European Jewry and we must be with them. Please do raise this matter with the War Office IMMEDIATELY and get men flown out here. We need help and more help.

After a protracted stay in the camp, the strain became evident to such an extent that Leslie Hardman was advised to leave and serve in a quieter area within the zone of occupation. He was posted to Lübeck where he continued with dedication to look after a group of Jews who had been found there.

With the removal of the dead from the huts, the task of preparing some form of hospitalisation was undertaken. Those who showed any sign of life expectancy were taken from the midst of the filth and transported to what became known as the 'human laundry' where they were deloused, washed, dusted with DDT, wrapped in clean blankets and admitted into an improvised hospital which comprised huts which had been thoroughly cleaned and made ready for their reception.

This proved inadequate as the numbers increased daily. The former *Wehrmacht* officer's mess, called the Roundhouse, was converted into a hospital run under the personal supervision of Brigadier Glynn Hughes, the Chief Medical Officer of the 2nd Army, a man who was to gain the respect and esteem of many hundreds who felt they owed their lives to his devotion and concern. He was a man of great proportions, both physically and spiritually. Though formidable in appearance, over six feet in height and solidly built, in his dealings with his patients he displayed warmth and gentleness. (See Appendix F, p. 134.)

Death and evacuation to hospital reduced the numbers in the camp, but still many remained whose physical condition was precarious. I well recall offering an inmate one of my dry biscuits which the recipient gleefully called 'cake'; a compliment to army rations, but of little use in such dire circumstances. The feeding problem was a priority, for it was not yet known what these starved bodies could digest. Soldiers, out of goodwill, had given them some of their rations, but all too often this proved fatal.

It was at this stage that a call was issued for British medical students to volunteer for famine relief. Under the supervision of a doctor who had had experience in the Bengal famine, the students were directed to administer what was called the 'Bengal Mixture'. This, I later learned, consisted of dried milk, flour and sugar, which soon proved both unsatisfactory and ineffectual. The mixture could not be digested, it was too rich and sweet.

Intravenous injections were also attempted, but these, too, were unsuccessful not merely from the viewpoint of their inherent quality, but because of the psychological effect of their application. Many of the inmates had memories of experiments carried out by the Nazis which involved injections, and were thus profoundly disturbed by the very thought of being subjected to such treatment.

It was at this juncture that I felt it essential to list the names of those who had survived their terrible ordeal. Going from hut to hut, I noted the names and the towns of origin of as many as could find the strength to convey the required information. The effort was utterly futile, as all too many of them would not enter the records of the living. In too many cases they died even as I spoke to them and would soon be destined to be interred in the mass graves. It was a heartbreaking experience only comparable to that of the medical staff who felt that they were fighting a losing battle.

Yet all the while we were being pestered by organisations back in England with the request that we provide them with lists of survivors. Their intention was honourable for they hoped that with the aid of such lists, families might be reunited. Little did they appreciate the conditions with which we had to contend.

Otto Schiff of the United Kingdom Research Bureau for German, Austrian and Stateless Persons from Central Europe wrote on 27 April:

> I have been in touch with Rabbi Brodie and he suggested that I might write to you and ask for your and your chaplains' co-operation in obtaining lists of names of Jews found in German territory now occupied by British forces.
>
> Whilst we have been receiving such lists through Chaplain Nadich covering American occupied territory, we have so far not received similar lists from the British Chaplains. Chaplain Nadich, whilst not being able yet to give us names of the Jewish inmates of the Buchenwald concentration camp, has informed us of the numbers and of the requests which a Jewish committee, which has been formed in the camp, has put forward. These requests will largely have to be dealt with by the Inter-Governmental Committee on Refugees, and I got in touch at once with Sir Herbert Emerson and also with Mr Anthony de Rothschild, chairman of the Central British Fund for Relief and Reconstruction which is making an appeal for £1,000,000 to assist in the building up of Jewish communal life on the Continent.
>
> I fully realise that your time must be fully occupied but I

should be most grateful if you could give us every assistance possible in the direction indicated.

I replied to him on 30 April.

Many thanks for yours of the 27th inst. There are a number of points which need clarification.

I do not know whether your organisation is interested in all European Jews and especially Eastern European. The majority of the inmates of Belsen are of this type. They number more than 25,000. Does your Committee have any influence regarding the future prospects of these poor people? The question '*Wohin?*' is being asked of us and we have no reply. What of the German Jews and their future? They are displaced persons since they have no home to return to nor can they think of returning to Germany. I would like some information on this point.

I would further like to add that so far we have not met any Jews outside this camp. The restrictions regarding contact with civilians are severe and we have not had the opportunity of searching for our brethren in those places which have not been taken by our forces. I have discussed the matter at length with Military Government officials at army headquarters and I have the right now to demand information from Burgermeisters when required. But we cannot cope with the work and cannot possibly comb through every town and village in Germany. We are only two chaplains in 2nd Army and until now our military commitments are heavy. I have appealled to Rabbi Brodie to send more chaplains especially for this work and the army is making the same demands. It is utterly fantastic. How can we possibly be of real help to our stricken brethren when we are so under-staffed.

Further with regard to lists. We are faced with a complete dilemma. I have in my possession now lists of men and women numbering in all some 3,000 which have been compiled with the help of a few people within the camps. I have a list of 2,000 men who are situated in the 'upper camp' i.e. Camp No. 2., and a list of some 900 women all of whom desire, quite rightly, to emigrate to Palestine. I further have a list of women of German origin numbering in all 46, and a few 'Aryans'. I cannot spare these lists yet because of some I have only one copy and I am devoting every moment of my spare time to copying them so that I can send them off elsewhere. Palestine and America should have copies since most of their relatives are in these countries. I have no clerical assistance to cope with all this. I am almost frantic with the work and keep appealing for help. As soon as I can make it I shall send the lists to you.

Further I have a batch of letters addressed to relatives in various parts of the world. Most of them are incompletely addressed since the people are not certain of the whereabouts of their relatives. I propose to send the letters addressed to England to your office in the hope that you can cope with this problem and arrange for the information to be extracted and lists published so that we can arrange a link up with relatives. I sincerely hope you can. It would be a great Mitzvah.

What of the Relief Teams? I have neither seen nor heard of them. Two chaplains cannot manage all this, and considering the difficulties under which we labour, more cannot be expected of us. We want to do more, but we need help.

I have to inform you that we are preparing for another camp to fall into British hands. Neuengamme will shortly be open to us and we expect to find similar conditions there. . . unless we are too late. Imagine, therefore, our position when we shall have one chaplain in each camp. I do not see how it will be done. We must have men here supported by teams of workers who will help in compiling information. Can you help us, please? Awaiting your immediate reply and asking your forgiveness if I sound aggressive. I am working at high pressure and under the most harrowing conditions.

In the midst of the realisation of the inadequacy of the services which could be rendered to these poor people, one unbelievable experience revived my sagging spirits. I chanced upon a hut in the women's section which, in contrast to the others, was spotlessly clean. It was inhabited by a group of young girls who, in their determination to survive, had ensured that they would care for their personal hygiene and remain free from infection. This group I learned, were late arrivals in Belsen and had not been subjected to the ordeals of the other inmates and were therefore in a better state of health. To my great delight they all spoke Hebrew fluently having been educated in a Hebrew school in Munkacz.

They were like a ray of sunshine dispersing the gloom of the camp. Their irrepressible spirits helped revive my own. We sat and spoke Hebrew, sang Hebrew songs and were imbued with the conviction that in spite of every effort to exterminate Jewry, the people of Israel lived. So we sang 'Am Yisrael Chai' with an added zest. At their invitation, I visited them again on a Shabbat and the Oneg Shabbat they organised was enhanced by a wonderful cake which they had baked. How they managed to find the ingredients I just could not imagine. To my utter amazement they had even decorated it with the words 'Li'chvod Ha'Oreach'.

I was deeply moved. Such a display of ingenuity and affection brought tears to my eyes. That Shabbat coincided with the weekly Sidrah which describes the venture of the twelve spies sent to investigate the contours of the Land of Israel. Having spent three years in the Middle East and knowing Palestine as I did, I talked to them about life in the country, the Yishuv, and the beauty of the landscape. There was no doubt in my mind that they were destined to go on Aliyah. They were well equipped to make a solid contribution once they received permission to emigrate.

The combination of a sound knowledge of Hebrew and their experiences during their incarceration, would make them ideal Olim. The one question which disturbed me and which I could not discuss with them was how and when would their hopes be realised and would they obtain the necessary certificates which the Mandatory Government of Palestine alone could allocate? Nor were they the only ones who were convinced that their ultimate destination was Palestine and expressed their wishes in no uncertain terms.

Hilda Greenbaum, one such girl, wrote to the London office of the Women's International Zionist Organisation:

> I wrote a letter to you some days ago, but I do not know whether or not it reached you.
>
> I am sure you have seen many reports on our conditions here, I am, therefore, passing it over in silence. We have suffered enough. What matters is, we are still living – very few of us in proportion to those of our people in Europe who were exterminated – very few, with the one goal before our eyes – our land.
>
> Therefore I appeal to you, try everything you can to help us as long as we have enough strength left in us to work for Palestine. Through Rev. Levy we were enlightened about many things and we are grateful to have found such a man here at this moment. We are certain that our way will be hard, but we do not shrink back from anything.
>
> We rely on you! We are working out a list of the Jewish girls of this camp which will be sent to you.

With the passing weeks, the task of evacuating the inmates from the camp proceeded apace. Those who survived had been transferred to the upper camp which became the largest hospital in Europe caring for some 15,000 patients.

The end of the death camp was in sight. On 21 May, exactly five weeks after the entry of the military, a team of Engineers equipped with flame throwers destroyed every trace of this hell to the relief of all those who had so strenuously fought against the ravages of diseases which had claimed so many victims.

3

Shortly after my letter of 26 April appeared in the *Jewish Chronicle* I wrote to the Assistant Chaplain General, my local superior in the Chaplain's Department. I deemed it essential that he should be aware of the problems which we Jewish Chaplains had to face now that concentration camps were being discovered. Whilst according to army regulations our first duty was to our own military flock, our religious loyalty demanded that we devote time and energy to our fellow Jews who were in such dire straits. I therefore felt duty bound to send him a memo in the hope that he would pass it on to higher authority and that my plea for additional assistance would produce a positive reply.

I was sure that by then he would have received information from military sources on the liberation of Belsen and the conditions which prevailed. What concerned me was that he should receive some insight into the Jewish perspective. I therefore emphasised that the Jewish inmates were of mixed nationalities originating from France, Belgium, Holland, a few from Germany but the vast majority were from Eastern Europe which reflected the enormity of Jewish suffering under the Nazis.

I also referred to the fact that so many had passed through other concentration camps before they reached Belsen. I did not belabour the physical privations which led to such appalling death tolls, certain as I was that this information would have been transmitted by the military medical services. My major concern was for the army to supply additional personnel to be made available to us.

Hence I wrote:

In view of the fact that we only have two Jewish Chaplains in the 2nd Army we urgently require more assistance. It is suggested that at least two more chaplains be made available in Belsen, one for each of the two camps. In addition, civilian groups of Jewish Relief Workers must be sent out forthwith. These workers to have a knowledge of first-aid, German, Yiddish and are to assist throughout the camp for all inmates. It is visualised that in the near future other such camps may be uncovered. Hence my dilemma being so under-manned. It is requested that the War Office be contacted forthwith and that the help be flown out to us without delay.

Information is available that of the many millions of Jews known to have existed in Central and Eastern Europe prior to 1933, more than five million have so far been exterminated by the Nazis. Those that we have discovered in Belsen are but a fraction of the remnant of those Jewries. They live in the permanent fear of repatriation to their countries of origin where it is known that anti-Semitism is still rife. The young people in particular have orientated their lives during the period of their incarceration to future emigration to Palestine. Were we to hint that such emigration is impossible they would readily hang themselves. It is a tragic fact that even within the camp anti-Semitism exists and Jews are suffering at the hands of their fellow victims. An immediate problem is created by the presence of several German Jews in the camp. Nothing has so far been said or written about their prospects. They cannot return to Germany nor can they be regarded as Displaced Persons. They are homeless in the fullest sense of the word. It is hoped that Military Government will give special attention to this problem and assist us to maintain their sagging morale.

Now that evacuation has commenced from Camp No. 1 to

No. 2, priority is being given to minority nations, i.e. French, Belgian and Dutch, but the majority are Eastern European and their evacuation is being delayed. In view of the fact that the youth within the camp are of the latter category I appeal that special consideration be given to the healthier ones among them to prevent their being stricken by the prevailing diseases and be forever lost to us.

Little did I realise then how complicated was the Relief issue. On 3 May I wrote to Mr Otto Schiff who also presided over the Jewish Relief Committee in London urging him to use his influence on the authorities. From him I learned of the existence of the Jewish Committee for Relief Abroad and that people were being trained for this work overseas, but were being hampered by official bureaucracy. No relief worker could be dispatched unless specifically asked for by the military authorities and the final word rested with Supreme Head-quarters Allied Expeditionary Forces based in Paris. Thus whilst the buck was passed from one source to another no material aid was forthcoming.

Then to my astonishment I was informed that members of a Jewish Relief Team were cooling their heels in Holland because there was insufficient work for them to do. To add to my growing amazement I learned that a Quaker team had been allowed into Belsen. In their ranks was a Jewess by the name of Jane Leveson. This delightful lady, whose dedication I later had reason to appreciate, had volunteered to serve, and not having received the facility under Jewish auspices, had joined up with the Quakers whose team was the first to be admitted to the camp.

Why should a non-Jewish Relief Team receive such pre-ference? Was there some insidious reason for excluding a Jewish team or was is a matter of chance? I had no alternative but to approach the authorities personally and not rely on an exchange of correspondence.

I therefore travelled to the Headquarters of Military Government in Brussels. There I met a young major and placed my request for the transfer of the Jewish team from Holland to become effective immediately. His response was to show me a map on which were a series of pins each indicating a camp that had been liberated by the Allied Forces. 'You see these places,' he said, 'there are so many that as far as we are concerned it is all purely academic.' I remember this response vividly and also my reply to him. 'They are dying like flies in Belsen and you sit here enjoying the luxury of Brussels and you have the audacity to say that this is merely academic. You will take immediate action or I will have no compunction but to take the matter up with higher authority.' With this outburst I left him and my anger must have been effective as on 17 May I received a letter from the Jewish Committee for Relief Abroad:

We do, of course, know of the tremendous work you are doing and of the conditions, as far as they are describable, in Bergen-Belsen. (We received a further report yesterday from Jane Leveson, who is one of our relief volunteers working in the camp with the Friends Relief Unit.)

We are very anxious that you should know what we are endeavouring to do and what we have succeeded in doing. As soon as Bergen-Belsen was liberated, we asked 21st Army Group, through the Council of British Societies for Relief Abroad, of which we are a constituent member and which is our contact with the military authorities, for our team in Holland to be transferred to Belsen. In spite of continual pressure we have not to date heard of the decision, although yesterday we heard through the leader of the team that they were to be sent to a camp in Germany. If this is the result of your approach, you have indeed done very well.

We have been trying unremittingly to get additional personnel and/or a team across. We have the people, and the difficulties are always technical and boil down to the need for a written request from the military authorities on the spot. There seems to be an unwillingness on the part of the military to use civilian relief workers and the authorities here – the Foreign

Office etc. – are holding their hands until such a request is made. If you could persuade the authorities on the spot to make such a request to the War Office in London, it would be a great contribution.

We have also offered a team of British Jewish Personnel comprising medical, social welfare and administrative sections, to go as such or be split up, for immediate service. We have the people – you push at your end to get them brought out. So far we have managed for the American Jewish Joint Distribution Committee to use five of our social welfare personnel in the various camps, but even for these the Ministry of Labour releases and exit permits are not yet through.

We are more than anxious that there should be no misunderstanding. Hence I mention the following details of letters written to you. Miss Joan Stiebel of the Jewish Refugees Committee, who works in close contact with us and is in this office every day, told us that she informed you of the dispatch of the team for Holland, in her first letter to you. In her second letter she told you that we were trying everything possible to get the team or individuals transferred to Belsen. Dr. Schonfeld, who is in charge of our department for religious reconstruction, we know has been in contact with you and has sent you some religious requisites.

We want to help you in every way possible.

At this stage of the war the army was making steady advance into Germany. I had to keep in constant contact with Head-quarters to which I was officially attached. This meant that I could not remain in Belsen but had to commute between the camp and H.Q. On my return to my Base I found a message waiting for me at the office of the Assistant Chaplain General to the effect that the army Chief of Staff had seen me in Belsen and was conscious that I needed help; would I therefore inform him of the number of additional chaplains I required to relieve the pressure. I was deeply touched by his solicitude and immediately replied that at least five would be needed.

Action was taken at once. My Senior Chaplain, Rabbi

Brodie, was requested by the War Office to select suitable candidates. On 3 May he wrote to me to say that this was in hand and that the Jewish Committee for Relief Abroad had a team of lay workers ready to leave – they were only awaiting the OK from Civil Affairs. I replied to him on 6 May:

> Many thanks for yours of the 3rd Inst. I shall welcome the arrival of Elton and Richards and have already requested that on their arrival in this theatre, that they be flown up to me and thus avoid undue delay. They will be sent to camps forthwith, one to Belsen and the other to Sandbostel which was uncovered a few days ago.
>
> For your information, I am forwarding all information regarding surviving Jews in these camps to the Search Bureau. Schonfeld has written asking for information in the name of the Association of Jewish Refugees. I am certain that I shall be inundated with requests of this type from all over the world. Already such requests are coming in from Italy and Palestine. I just cannot cope with it all.
>
> I am perturbed about the suggestion that civilian ministers be sent over here to work in the camps. I most heartily disapprove. They will have no status with the army and no approach to higher military authority. The chaplain in uniform has influence in such places and can do inestimable work within the sphere of Mil. Govt. I think it would be disastrous if we could not find chaplains to come over and it says little for the department as a whole.
>
> I sincerely trust that Elton and Richards have been instructed to report to me and that they should work under my direction. I have been and am being consulted by the authorities here on all kinds of subjects connected with the occupation and the camps. I do not wish that these chaplains, who are 'green' to overstep the mark and make unnecessary complications.
>
> I would point out that the occupational scheme for Germany is worthy of our attention. I do not know whether you intend to maintain the chaplaincy at home at its present strength, but I do feel most strongly that we should receive more attention over here. The British Zone of Occupation has been defined

and the territory is vast. Bearing in mind that we shall have to commence a search for individual Jews who may have survived and who may have sailed under false colours for so long and will soon come out into the open, as they did in the Netherlands, chaplains will be needed to help in this direction too.

I must confess that never before have I felt so alone in my work. Your long absence from the office has forced me to rely entirely on my own resources and the periodic word from your clerk, able though he is, has left me in complete darkness as to our future in this theatre.

When they arrived the chaplains proved to be a strange assortment indeed. Three of them were dressed in the uniform of the Jewish Committee for Relief Abroad and two were army chaplains. To impose military discipline on them was, therefore, impossible. Rabbi Dr E. Munk, Rabbi to an ultra orthodox congregation whom I had known in London was a genuine hard-working man whom I posted to Celle in Hanover where a group of survivors was sited. Rabbi Vilensky was posted to the upper camp. He was later to prove a liability rather than a help. The third was a Rabbi Baumgarten, a Chassid whose side curls were, with difficulty, concealed under his cap. He, too, was somewhat of a misfit and caused quite an uproar in his relations with the inmates of the upper camp. The other two were British trained clerics: Reverend Richards was an army chaplain who did a superb job throughout the period of his stay in Germany. He was dedicated to the task and proved a most reliable and loyal colleague. The Reverend Elton, however, gave me cause to reprimand him severely. He had been born in Hungary and moved to England in his adolescence. Among the inmates were a number of Hungarian Jews and it was to them that, in my view, he displayed disproportionate attention. I had to convince him that our duty was to be impartial and all were to be treated with equal concern. In due course I removed him from Belsen and sent him to Braunschweig where a group of survivors had assembled.

On some nights I arrived so late in my room, and was so exhausted, that I just could not write to my wife. I could only apologise to her the following day.

8 May 1945

. . . I wish I did not have such a one track mind. I think of the declaration of VE day and realise how empty it all sounds and how void of any content. I suppose that in the mess tonight there will be a fair amount of drinking and merriment and I just do not know how to face it. The order has come out that today and tomorrow will be celebrated by giving the staff of H.Q. a half holiday but a skeleton staff must be on duty still. One cannot down tools and think that all is over. There will be Thanksgiving services and moments perhaps of serious thought.

But my mind revolves around Belsen and the work which has to be done there to restore so many tens of thousands of people to health and normality. I just cannot get the co-operation I need to put things in order. I have been asking for lists of the Jews in the camp and all the promises that have been made to me have not been fulfilled. I am being inundated with requests for information. Families are searching for relatives. I have not the information yet and cannot get people to work. I have appealed to the healthier ones to help me but they just think mainly of themselves. poor wretches I cannot blame them.

Whilst there yesterday I met two men from Hanover who are members of the Jewish Committee of that town. They are the last remaining men of a once large *Arbeits-Lager*. They have formed a committee and gave me the list of their names. They also informed me that there are 70 Jews in the town who have never been in a concentration camp and who have been unmolested. Apparently the Gestapo in Hanover was not so severe with them. I have not the time to go down and see them and a chance visit for an hour is not good enough. One must be prepared to spend time there and to see conditions on the spot and interview people. How can we do all this when I am alone for outside work. Now I have to arrange meetings for the troops on the occasion of the VE celebrations and services have to be held. I do it with little heart knowing that whatever can be done for these people should take pride of place. I should have a number of chaplains whom I can send out as soon as I hear of a group of survivors. A sort of Flying Squad. I have the ideas and know what I want but cannot get the help. It is an appalling state of affairs and no one seems to realise what it is all about. I have had a long conversation with the Commandant of Belsen about the formation of a Jewish transit camp for those who do not desire to return to the countries of their origin. He is all sympathy and now I have to fight it out with Military government authorities. My opinion of the latter is beyond description. It could not be lower. I am sure that the throwouts of the army have been given jobs in this department. And we expect to govern Germany with such people...

One small diversion which I know will please you. This afternoon at tea in the mess we had three naval guests all of whom had been prisoners of war and recently released. They are waiting return to U.K. and as they are near here we invited them in to tea. This evening we had them and five others in to dinner and I was asked to speak and toast them. The first time that this has happened and that I should be asked pleased me immensely. They are a grand set of chaps and have all had a hell of a time. To think that on VE night we should be able to entertain such fellows is pleasing and nothing could be more appropriate. Don't you agree?

But hilarity is lacking in the mess tonight. The officers are not drinking and no one will get soused. They feel tired and long for home and families and, God, so do I. There is a celebration for the men here. A large bonfire and beer and fireworks but I have no desire to go along and see the fun, if one can call it that. I sit here and think of you and long and yearn to see you and our son. Thank God you are safe from the perils of war now. That you can sleep at nights without fear of bombs and rockets. Every time the mail was delayed I wondered and worried about you. Dreading the evil possibilities.

Good night my dearest and God bless you. May the day of real rejoicing come soon.

and on 9 May 1945:

. . . I have had a hell of a day again and so many high hopes have been dashed to the ground as a result of an interview which I had with the Brigadier at Main Army H.Q. I asked to see him and he realised it was about the Belsen Camp. I was called to place my proposals before a special meeting which he was holding with heads of departments and I received no satisfaction. On the contrary after the meeting he saw me privately and informed me in no uncertain terms that my first duty lay towards the men of the army 'that was what I was paid for' and that though humanity was involved at the camps, I was not to devote all my time to them. I explained that we are only two chaplains and that one is there all the time and I have to help and there is so much to do but he was adamant. Imagine how I feel. Now I am being swamped with letters from everywhere . . . I need a staff of twenty to deal with it. The people back there do not realise it and even those who should know cannot understand. I feel that all my pleas are in vain and they make me so heart-broken. How can I do all this when I cannot organise the people in the camp? They think of food and themselves first and last and when I try to get them to give me information they crack up on me. They are not in a fit state to help me and no help comes from outside.

And now the army demands that I devote all my time to the troops and leave this alone. They do not see our problem and the Jewish angle does not receive attention. I have placed a scheme before them for a Jewish Transit Camp for these people and thus prevent them from being sent off with their co-nationals. The Poles hate the Jews still and anti-Semitism is visible in the camp itself amongst the victims. Can I be more explicit? I said this at the meeting this evening and they could not understand. They talk of 'victimisation' and they understand by that only bloodshed.

They do not know what the Polish methods are. Remember the 'Szid' expression with all its adjectives? They are heard there still. Can I make them understand? I talk of food and they feel that I am speaking from bias. The diet is not good enough and the people can't eat the food and the Brigadier tells me that he hates bully beef but has had to eat it for five years. Is that an answer? Has he or any of them ever known what hunger is? Tonele, I feel at times that I am fighting a losing battle. I am surrounded on all sides by people who will not understand me and now London does not come to our aid either.

4

WITH THE TOTAL destruction of Camp No. 1 – the death camp, all attention was directed to Camp No. 2, which I have called the upper camp. As a large part of it had been converted to provide for the essential hospitalisation of the sick, the remainder became hopelessly overcrowded. The Military Government authorities in their anxiety to reduce the numbers, particularly of those who were comparatively fit to travel, proceeded to classify the inmates according to their countries of origin with a view to their repatriation.

At that time the nationalities of the inmates varied considerably. There were French, Belgian, Dutch, Poles, Hungarians and a few Germans. The French, Belgian and Dutch were all too eager to be restored to their former countries, but the Poles, Hungarians and Germans demanded special treatment. Jews who originated from Poland would, under no circumstances, return there for obvious reasons. The few German Jews were conscious that were they to be repatriated they would be treated as enemy aliens. As for the Hungarian Jews, realising their own special needs, they took it upon themselves to address a special plea to the Senior Military Government Officer of the British Liberation Army, a copy of which they passed to me:

30 May 1945

Sir,

We, the elected representatives of all Jews in Belsen coming
from Hungary and Transylvania, humbly present this petition.

Our only crime in the eyes of the Nazis was that we were
Jews and as such were made to suffer slavery, torture and even
extermination. We were deported from our homes in March
1944 and have passed through the hell of the concentration
camps of Eastern Europe. Many of us no longer have any
knowledge of the whereabouts of our families and loved ones.
Husbands, wives and children have been cruelly separated.
Many of us know that members of our families have been
exterminated in Auschwitz and other camps.

From the depths of our misery we prayed for the day when
the Allied Forces would deliver us. That day came when the
British Forces over-ran Belsen and delivered us from the
suffering which we have endured for so long.

We are now faced with the tragic problem of rehabilitation.
We are homeless and without council. It has been said that we
are still to be considered as enemies of the Allies since the
countries from which we were deported have fought against the
Allies and that therefore we are not entitled to the protection of
our liberators.

It is because we are Jews and have been made to suffer that
we humbly claim your protection. Our suffering is, at least,
comparable to that of the victims among the Allied nations. We
have not joined forces with the enemies of Britain or her Allies
and our casualties as Jews may well be compared to those fallen
on the field of honour. We have suffered as Jews not as
Hungarians.

In the name of all those whose voice we express we plead
that we be treated as the victims of war and the ideology of the
Nazis and that we receive the same treatment as is offered to all
those who have been liberated by the Allies from the hell of
Belsen.

This plea was eloquently and touchingly expressed but I
harboured the gravest doubts as to the response that might be

forthcoming. From my contacts with the Military Government I gained the impression that all would not be plain sailing. The issue of repatriation was complex and those of us who would become involved in it would have to face severe obstacles. Knowing that the Military Government Detachment in charge of Belsen was not the final arbiter and that policy instructions would have to come from a higher source, on 16 May I wrote to a Mr T. T. Scott of the Displaced Persons Section of the United Nations Relief and Rehabilitation Administration then sited in London.

> I am taking the liberty of writing to you in order to bring to your notice a number of problems affecting the Jews in the Belsen camp.
>
> I am sure it would be needless to bring to your attention the appalling conditions which we found on our entry into the camp. I have been working there for some time now and I regret to say that even though the military are doing all they can to restore the wretched inmates to physical recovery, their mental anxieties are far from allayed. There are some 20,000 Jews there, and possibly more, whose nationalities vary according to the countries from which they were deported. The vast majority are Eastern Europeans.
>
> It is self evident that the majority of these Jews cannot return to the countries of their origin. They fear a resurgence of the same ideology which brought them to this present impasse. The youth in particular see no future in their former countries. They have oriented their much-dreamed-of future to settlement in Palestine, which is the obvious solution for them. Some desire to return to their countries of origin in the hope that they may find some trace of their families. But this is only a temporary measure. They are determined that their final destination is Palestine.
>
> Meanwhile, the great problem is the immediate future facing them and us. Very shortly the first great exodus from Belsen will take place under the auspices of the Military authorities. The usual D.P. channels will be brought into play. The evacuees from Belsen will be passed through various camps

according to their nationalities. The great 'Drang nach Osten' [desire for expansion eastwards] may be enacted.

I have urged that the Jewish victims of the Nazis deserve special consideration. I feel most strongly that a Jewish Transit Camp should be opened with all possible haste to which all Jews who do not desire to be repatriated should be sent, there to remain until the powers that be can arrive at a decision which will define their status and future. I am sure that organisations such as yours would sympathise with such a suggestion.

I would further suggest that the ideal site for such a Transit Camp is Hanover, where the inmates of the local camp are well organised. I am assured that there is ample accommodation for a considerable number of Jews. There is an excellent agricultural school in the area where youth could be trained for work on the land.

Another problem which faces us is the future of the German Jewish nationals in Belsen. Some of them have already been sent out of the camp with a mere pittance in their pockets. They will now wander over the countryside in the vain attempt to search for their families and a source of livelihood. I see little prospect for such people who have spent so many years in concentration camps. Surely they deserve special consideration.

I appeal to you and to your vast organisation to come to our aid. Can any pressure be brought to bear to expedite the establishment of Jewish Transit Camps? I cannot do more than stress the point with the Military, but they wait for instructions from above – the usual Military procedure. Were an order given they would obey it. From the depths of desperation in Belsen I most earnestly appeal to you to do everything possible to help this last relic of European Jewry.

My proposal that a Jewish Transit Camp be established was not accepted. This was a bitter disappointment for it would have saved a great deal of heartache for the many hundreds who would have welcomed the segregation and it would have afforded protection from the blatant anti-Semitism which existed even in the horror camp where, we were reliably informed, Jews were deprived of food and exposed to insults from Polish and Hungarian non-Jews.

What then was to be the status of those who refused to be repatriated, the majority of whom were Polish Jews? How could the authorities be convinced that they must be assigned a special category? I contended that they should be regarded as stateless for this would protect them against the pressure from Polish Liaison officers who attempted to persuade the authorities that they were Polish citizens and must therefore be treated as such. It was indeed a great relief when the Military Government issued the following order: 'United Nations personnel other than identified Soviet Citizens or war criminals will not be repatriated against their wishes.'

This of course, dealt only with the non-repatriation aspects of the problem, and left open the question of actual status. The term 'stateless' had not yet been clarified and therefore hundreds of Polish Jews remained in a limbo of undefined identity.

5

In previous communications I had expressed concern for German Jews and how they would be treated by the victorious Allies. With the cessation of hostilities and the collapse of the German army, the road to Berlin was now open. This afforded the opportunity to visit the Jewish military personnel stationed there and to ascertain whether Jewish civilian survivors might be found.

Berlin was in a state of total devastation – the result of ceaseless bombardment to which it had been subjected, especially by the Russians. To ride down the once handsome tree-lined Unter den Linden was like passing along the highway of a ghost city.

The people looked haggard and bedraggled, fearful of the presence of so many Russian troops who dominated the city. The few children looked pale and hopelessly underfed. I well recall an incident which still lingers hauntingly in my memory; I was sitting in my jeep when a small child approached me, and stretching out his hand appealed to me, '*Herr Major, haben sie Schokolate?*' Fortunately I had some with me and without hesitation gave it to him. Not for a moment could I transfer my loathing of the Germans to this poor hungry mite, who, for all I knew, might be the son of a German soldier responsible for some atrocity against one of my people. The sins of the fathers cannot be visited on the children, not even in such a place as Berlin, once the generating station for so much Jewish suffering.

Amidst this devastation I could not envisage that any Jewish institution had survived the terrible onslaught. All the synagogues had been destroyed so we were led to believe, not by Allied bombardment but on that dreadful *Kristallnacht*, when Nazi fury was unleashed on the community and its institutions. Yet to my intense delight I learned that Shabbat services were being held in converted halls attached to the ruined Pestalozzi and Joachinsthaler synagogues. Here were gathered groups who had survived incarceration at Theresienstadt and had recently returned to their native city. I joined the worshippers in their improvised synagogue. The service was simple and most moving.

From them I learned of the wealth of Sifrei Torah which were once in the possession of the Gemeinde. Four hundred had been buried in the Jewish cemetery and fortunately none had been damaged by this interment and would soon be used again if and when the communities could be revived.

I naturally asked these people what they desired most, and the answer was identical from every one of them – *Auswanderung* – they could not remain in Berlin or in any part of Germany. It was the graveyard of their families and of their hopes for the future. There was no hope of retrieving their possessions or of rebuilding their shattered lives. They feared the effects of Nazi propaganda which had penetrated deeply into the soul of the German people but which lay dormant for the time being. They faced starvation resulting from the regulations governing the distribution of food. They felt unwanted. They had relatives abroad, in Palestine, England and America, if only they could join them, but they felt trapped.

The only way I could allay their fears and anxieties was to act as an intermediary in helping them to make contact with the outside world. I therefore urged them to write letters to any relative they might have anywhere in the world and I would collect them on the following day and arrange for their despatch. On returning to my base I sorted out all these letters according to the countries of the addressees. Those for England were sent to the U.K. Search Bureau, for Palestine to the Jewish Agency, and for the U.S.A. to the World Jewish Congress. In each case I requested that every effort be made to ensure that the addressees be found by whatever means possible. I felt that I had performed the greatest Mitzvah in helping to create a living link between these survivors and their families.

Little did I realise at that time what the repercussions of such action would be. Several weeks later I received a message that the Assistant Chaplain General wished to see me on an urgent matter. It transpired that one of the addressees had written to a relative in Switzerland to the effect that a letter had been received from Berlin and that future communication with the sender could be made through me, giving my name and military address. By sheer accident this letter had been intercepted by Military Intelligence who reported the matter to my superiors for necessary action to be taken against me.

I was reprimanded very severely by the A.C.G. and accused of contravening security regulations. In my response I asked him whether he was addressing me as a superior officer or whether I might speak to him as one cleric to another. 'Of course I am primarily a priest,' he replied. I then pointed out to him that these wretched people could not possibly have any military secrets to impart. All they desired was to make contact with close relatives to inform them that they were alive. Surely it was a basic humanitarian act on my part to assist in the reunification of families. In justification of the reprimand all this cleric could say was, 'The trouble with you, Levy, is that you are a Jewish nationalist.' I would have liked to respond by thanking him for the compliment, but I refrained and with that the incident was closed. At least I enjoyed the satisfaction of knowing that all the batches of letters dispatched from my office were on their way to their desired destination. (See Appendix D, p. 127.)

6

The Jewish Refugees' Committee wrote to me on 23 May to tell me of their efforts regarding relief workers:

1. The American Joint Distribution Committee have permission from SHAEF, Paris, to send a number of workers into the camps and have asked us to supply men and women. The authorities here, however, still will not give permission for the five people we have ready and waiting to go until they get a signal from Paris which has not yet come through. The Joint are urging it from their end and also from their London office here, if only we can just get this signal through all will be well.

2. The Jewish Committee for Relief Abroad is a member of the Council of British Societies for Relief Abroad which is the co-ordinating organisation for relief work in this country and covers all societies sending people out. The Council of Voluntary Societies is trying to get permission for the J.C.R.A. to be allowed to send an advance party of five really experienced people to Belsen or Lingen, wherever you want them. These might form the advance part of a team and it would have the advantage that they could come direct to you and would not have to wait about as the team in Holland has done for instruction as to where to go. Yesterday I went to see the High Commissioner for Refugees who is also the Director of Inter-Governmental Committee – this is responsible for all

the stateless people and those who are unwilling or unable to return to their own countries – and he is trying to help us in getting people out really quickly. I left him copies of your two letters and I know he will do everything he can to be helpful.

If we can get this wretched permission through do you not agree with me that it is better to send really first class social workers rather than teams which include four drivers?

Please keep on pushing at your end and you can rely on us this end to do everything we can to send you the best we can.

In response, and in order to expedite the granting of permission for relief workers to be sent to Germany, I wrote to the Military Government's Officer Commanding Civil Affairs on 21 May:

... These groups have been standing by for some time and not a word has been received from the authorities asking for their transfer.

The need is most urgent. The problems are growing daily. The Jews especially are most wretched as a result of their long and tortuous incarcerations. The reaction to the first flush of freedom and liberation has set in and the need for experienced men and women who understand them and speak to them in their own language is most urgent.

I would beg of you to do all in your power to obtain their permission to come over. So far only the Jewish chaplains have been attending to the needs of these poor people and we cannot manage without additional help.

Forgive my pressure but I cannot overstate the urgency for action to be taken.

Meanwhile events were moving rapidly in Belsen which was now declared a Displaced Persons' camp housing several thousand non-repatriated Jews, the majority of whom originated from Poland, Hungary and Transylvania. It soon became obvious that they needed to create some form of representative body which would act on their behalf in any negotiation with the powers that be. Thus, there came into being on 24 June, the Central Jewish Committee which would serve as the recognised 'spokesman' for all Jewish inmates irrespective of their country of origin. In due course the Committee became a semi-autonomous body. It created its own internal administration comprising a number of departments each specialising in distinct activities deemed essential for the welfare of all Jewish D.P.s wherever they were to be found. These departments were listed in the Committee's report dated 25 September which also stated that the Committee served to represent the whole of the British Zone of Occupation and was in contact with the American Zone. The titles and function of the departments were:

THE PRAESIDIUM comprising the Chairman, Yossel Rosensaft, Dr Hadassah Bimko and Berl Loifer. As the official representatives of the Committee they were to oversee the work of the departments and assume responsibility for all contacts with the 'outside world'.

THE SECRETARIAT which would undertake the registration of all arrivals at the camp, compile accurate statistics indicating the numbers who wished to return to their country of origin, and the numbers of children in various camps of given ages.

A RECORD ROOM in which the 98 centres in which Jews were to be found were to be listed and from which circulars, prepared for distribution, would be issued.

INFORMATION to assist in the search for relatives who may be found in the various centres in the British and American zones. To this end a card index of survivors was to be compiled in the hope of ultimately publishing a comprehensive list of all D.P.s.

STORES from which clothing and amenities would be distributed to selected cases, especially to the children and the sick in hospitals.

CULTURE   The presence in the camp of Chaim Feder, a well-known Yiddish artiste, led to the formation of a theatrical group which presented plays and recitals in the camp. This department also encouraged inmates to write diaries and compose poems and songs which would reflect the life and experiences of the inmates.

EDUCATION   In spite of the shortage of text books, courses were to be organised on such subjects as Hebrew, English, mathematics and art. Special attention to be given to the school opened in collaboration with the Jewish Relief Team.

PRESS   Attempts were made to produce a camp newspaper entitled *Unsere Shtimme* [Our Voice]. (Only three issues appeared due to the difficulties experienced in continuing such a costly undertaking.)

HEALTH   Each block in the camp to be scrupulously watched to ensure its hygienic condition was maintained. The hospitals to be regularly visited and amenities distributed to the patients.

CHILDREN AND YOUTH   In addition to the children's home, established to house some 30 orphan children between the ages of 10 to 14, every encouragement was to be given to the various Zionist movements, both religious and secular, which developed in the camp.

Under the dynamic and often uncompromising leadership of Yossel Rosensaft, the Committee operated most efficiently. Yossel, without doubt, was a unique personality. Before he reached Belsen he had been incarcerated in other concentration camps, suffered severely at the hands of his tormentors, but proved indestructible. His energy was formidable and his able leadership was acknowledged throughout the camp, and even beyond its confines. His manner of approach to the Military authorities was extraordinary. He regarded it as a matter of principle to address them in Yiddish, the language of the people he represented. Invariably he was accompanied by Norbert Wolheim, an able lieutenant, who acted as his interpreter. Norbert was German by birth but he identified himself whole-heartedly with his Eastern European fellow Jews whom his former compatriots would have slightingly called '*Ost Juden*'.

Once the Committee opened its own office, staffed by selected inmates, it sent its emissaries to wherever Jews were to be found in order to report back on the prevailing conditions. Thus, in the course of time, the Committee became the acknowledged representative body on behalf of all Jewish D.P.s in the British Zone.

Whilst Yossel and his Committee were engaged in 'political' activity, a fellow member of the Praesidium, Hadassah Bimko, directed her talents and energy not only to supervising the hygienic conditions in the camp but to rendering valuable assistance to Brigadier Glynn Hughes. Her earlier medical training and her linguistic talents were invaluable to him for she could communicate with the patients with facility. In this respect she was of greater use than the German doctors and nurses who were recruited to help in the hospital which by now was the biggest in Europe. She and Yossel worked in the closest harmony, an association which, we knew, would result in a happy and fruitful partnership. That they ultimately married came as no surprise.

7

EVERY TIME I returned to Belsen from a visit to installations in other parts of the British Zone, I invariably experienced a profound shock. Towards the end of May, when I was back again in the camp, I learned, to my horror, that over a thousand Jewish inmates had been transferred to Lingen, a township on the Dutch border, the purpose of which was ostensibly to relieve the pressure of over-population in Belsen and to provide extra hospital accommodation. Many of these transferees had recently been released from hospital and were hardly fit to undertake such a long and arduous journey in open lorries.

A relief worker and the Reverend Richards accompanied them. The report they submitted was devastating. Not only were the physical conditions of the journey harrowing, but on arrival the accommodation provided proved disgracefully inadequate. Lingen had been declared a camp for stateless Displaced Persons but in fact was to house many hundreds of Poles, Russians and others, and the Jews would have to live in close proximity to them.

Two weeks after the arrival of the Jews a census of Lingen's population was taken. The total number of inmates was 5676, comprising 2336 Russians; 2086 Poles; 8 Italians; 2 Dutch; 63 Yugoslavs; 24 Czechs; 5 Belgians; 1127 Jews from Belsen and 25 others.

In order to ascertain the true situation for myself, I visited Lingen and reported my findings and conclusions to the D.P. Section, Military Government at Army H.Q.

I have just returned from a four day stay at Lingen and submit this report on the condition of this 'stateless' camp. It can be summed up as APPALLINGLY INADEQUATE.

ARRIVAL OF D.P.S   1,127 Jews were dispatched from Belsen on Thursday, 24th May at 1230 hours and arrived at Lingen at 2200 hours. The Officer in charge of the local Military Government Detachment received warning of their impending arrival in the late evening of 23rd May. After a long and uncomfortable journey the D.P.s arrived in a state of exhaustion. Several of them had only just been discharged from Belsen hospitals.

CAMP CONDITIONS   On arrival the D.P.s were shown to five wooden huts which is their present accommodation. There is still no electricity laid on. No beds had been provided and the huts were filthy. A battle had taken place in this area and the scars were still visible. Not one of the huts is whole. Gaping holes in the sides and roofs admit rain and cold winds. THE HUTS ARE A REPLICA OF THOSE IN CAMP NO.1. IN BELSEN. The mental association of the D.P.s with that horror camp is obvious. Their first reaction was that they were being sent back to a concentration camp. Sanitation is bad. Emergency latrines – without seats – have been dug. No door has any form of lock. No inmate can enjoy any privacy.

Bedding has been obtained from the locality but the D.P.s still only have one blanket to cover themselves. No chairs or forms have been provided. Planks laid over petrol tins are improvised seating accommodation.

SEGREGATION OF THE `STATELESS´   The camp contains several thousand Poles and Russians and a variety of other nationalities. The existing stone barracks have been allocated to them whilst the Jews have to endure the decrepit huts. The Jewish D.P.s are constantly exposed to the 'propaganda' of the Poles and Russians which adds to their mental discomfiture. Any fraternisation which exists is entirely due to the fact that many of the Jewish D.P.s are young girls who have been deprived of the company of the male sex for a considerable time. The moral consequences are obvious and decidedly unhealthy.

FOOD   The constant reference to the calorie content of the food given to these D.P.s is misleading and even dishonest. The fact is that one half of the total calorific value of their diet is contained in the quarter of a loaf of bread which they receive daily. For the most part this bread has proven uneatable.

HEALTH   The only medical service available is via UNRRA. The hospital block in the Jewish Section contains 89 patients, 50 have already been sent to a hospital at Bedburg. These D.P.s are not fit to live in such conditions.

SUGGESTION   It is recommended that special villages be selected for these Stateless D.P.s and that the German occupants be ordered to vacate. Similar to Bedowick and elsewhere where Poles are installed. These people must be given facilities where rest and recuperation can only be achieved in pleasant surroundings. Houses should be allocated in these villages and a semblance of family life be created. IT IS OBVIOUS THAT LINGEN HAS PROVED A GHASTLY FAILURE.

In this report I did not elaborate on the word 'propaganda'. What actually happened was that a Polish liaison officer attached to the camp constantly put pressure on the Jews to declare that they were Polish citizens with the view to their future repatriation to Poland. This very thought horrified them for under no circumstances would they entertain the idea of returning to what they knew was the graveyard of their people.

The food problem was not unique to Lingen. The same complaint could be heard in Belsen. The emphasis on calorific value was ludicrous. If half of the calories was in the uneatable bread, what possible nourishment could be derived from the prescribed diet. All too often the cry was heard, 'Give us food not calories.' The authorities must have realised that as a result of such a deficient diet the inmates who were capable of doing so would find the means of sustaining themselves by 'organising' supplementary rations. That meant foraging in the surrounding countryside and stealing whatever they could lay their hands on. My suggestion that Jewish D.P.s be segregated from others and that they be housed in villages whose inhabitants should be evacuated was, I knew, somewhat extreme in its implications, but since it had been put into operation on behalf of the Poles, I saw no reason why it should not be repeated on behalf of the Jews.

In addition to the facts on which my recommendations were made, and which were based on my personal observation, much information was gleaned from verbal reports passed to me by Jane Leveson of the Quaker Relief Team who accompanied the inmates in their transfer from Belsen and who did outstanding work in the camp, and from Miss Roberts, a Red Cross Staff Officer and representative of the Council of the British Society for Relief Abroad. It was therefore not a biased report emanating from a prejudiced viewpoint but based on independent evidence submitted by professional relief workers.

It soon transpired that the Lingen experiment, if I can call it that, proved to be disastrous and this was even admitted by Major Grellan, the officer in charge of the Military Government Detachment responsible for running the camp. As a result the Jewish D.P.s were on the move again, transferred to another site, to Diepholz, in the vicinity of Osnabrück.

Jane Leveson and Chaplain Richards had visited the site in advance of the transfer and their reaction was far from favourable. The accommodation here, too, consisted of huts, reminiscent of Belsen. The number of beds was at least 800 short of the requirement. There was no indoor sanitation and washing facilities were lamentably inadequate.

As for electricity, whilst the fixtures were there, no light bulbs had been provided. It was evident from the outset that Diepholz would offer no solution and that dissatisfaction would soon lead to a further upheaval for the inmates. Another experiment had failed. The authorities, therefore, transported the Jewish D.P.s back to Belsen there to be reunited with former comrades. Their return was welcomed by the Central

Jewish Committee which would henceforth minister to their needs as far as they could.

These attempts to relieve the pressure caused by over-population were, from the viewpoint of the Military authorities, understandable, as the need to find additional hospital accommodation became increasingly urgent. But whilst the intention was good, the practical application left much to be desired. Thus Lingen and Diepholz served as examples of poor planning and lack of foresight.

A similar disaster could have occurred at another camp to which Belsen inmates had been transferred had not action been taken in time to repair the damage. Some 1100 Polish Jewish D.P.s had been sent to Celle, 25 kilometres from Belsen. This camp was situated in a former German military college which comprised two large brick buildings in one of which the Jews were housed. There were insufficient beds and bunks. The rooms were far from clean due to a shortage of cleaning materials, and there were no cooking or eating utensils. The daily diet was that generally offered to inmates of the camps – a quarter of a loaf of black bread, an inferior potato soup and ersatz coffee.

This deficient diet led to the inevitable consequences. The inmates looted the farms in the neighbourhood. Jane Leveson reported that on visiting the camp she found the cooking of chickens, meat and vegetables in progress in various bedrooms. There seemed to be no way of controlling these foraging expeditions in the locality which presented the Military Government and the UNRRA officials with severe problems. It certainly contributed to the unpopularity of the D.P.s in the eyes of the official administration.

These looting operations became a regular practice even in Belsen which caused me great concern. I well recall addressing a meeting when I urged that the inmates refrain from this activity. In my best Yiddish I put it to them thus – 'At the moment you refer to it as "organising", but if you permit it to become a regular practice it will become second nature to you.

The time will come when it will be revealed in its true character – just plain "genevah" – stealing, a criminal offence. Why not stop it now!' I doubt whether I made much of an impression for their response was 'We are only getting our entitlement. The Germans took everything we had. Now we are only taking what is due to us.'

Meanwhile, the primitive conditions in the Celle camp began to improve. The Red Cross sent parcels and UNRRA undertook to supply the necessary amenities. Two Jewish Relief workers were posted to the camp and they both did a superb job. One was Rabbi Dr E. Munk who, with typical 'Yekkish' precision became an excellent organiser; the other was Mrs Rose Henriques who had had much experience in social work in London. She was a formidable lady. Although her religious outlook was totally different from that of Rabbi Munk, she worked with him most amicably, each having a profound respect for the other's devotion to the task. Her one weakness was her inability or unwillingness to appreciate the role which Palestine played in the sentiments of the inmates, which resulted at times in a display of antagonism towards her. With the improvements in conditions the Celle camp attracted a considerable influx of D.P.s. Their registration, supervised by Rabbi Munk, resulted in the publication of a comprehensive list of all inmates, classified according to previous nationality, giving their full name, date of birth and town of origin.

The printed booklet appeared in July under the title *She'erit Ha'Pletah in Celle*, and reflected the meticulous care with which the statistics were gathered and collated. We thus learnt that at the time there were 1257 Polish Jews; 364 Romanians; 220 Czechs; 119 Hungarians; 122 Greeks; and 52 Germans. It stated, however, that by the time the booklet went into print the Greeks and most of the Czechs had been repatriated.

8

AFTER SPENDING TWO months in hectic activity commuting between Belsen and Army H.Q. I was granted leave to return to London. But it was no holiday and nor did my family gain much pleasure from our reunion. Almost the whole of my time was spent in pleading the cause of Belsen's inmates. I addressed several meetings in synagogues where I appealed for clothing and other amenities to be sent to the Central Jewish Committee in the hope that the response would be commensurate with the need.

Of greater significance was the meeting which I had with Sir Herbert Emerson, the High Commissioner for Refugees, to whom I conveyed verbal pictures of the conditions prevailing in the camp. I laid special emphasis on the hopes and aspirations of the younger elements stressing that all, without exception, desired to go to Palestine, the only country that could and would absorb them. I told him that were I to return to Belsen without an assurance that Aliyah was possible, I might find them hanging from the rafters in their huts. Their desperation was such that life would have no meaning for them except in the land of their dreams.

He listened to me most attentively and, as I thought then, with sympathy, but his response was far from favourable. He appreciated my dilemma and that of these young people, but pleaded that such a solution to the problem was not within his competence. Emigration to Palestine was dependent on the number of certificates made available by the Mandatory authorities in Palestine. On a matter of such delicacy, he could bring no influence to bear.

I left him having achieved nothing positive. I could only hope that perhaps I had sown the seeds of an idea with him which might, in time, produce something advantageous. Little did he know that the young Zionists in Belsen would not wait for his intervention or for any official permission to proceed on Aliyah, but at an opportune moment would follow the 'underground' route through Europe to the ports and ships which would facilitate their 'illegal' immigration.

Equally significant but frustrating was a meeting held at New Court, the head office of the House of Rothschild, under the chairmanship of Mr Anthony de Rothschild. Present were leading representatives of Anglo-Jewry who, for the first time, were afforded an eye-witness account of the appalling conditions with which the liberators of Belsen had to contend. In precise details I described what I and my colleague had seen, the efforts made by the medical staff to combat the diseases which raged in the camp, and the difficulties experienced in obtaining the services of Relief Teams. I was convinced that they must have seen the report which I had sent to the *Jewish Chronicle*, yet all I could ascertain from them was that they were unaware of the true situation.

Even more devastating was the reaction of the representatives of the Zionist Federation who also pleaded ignorance. I knew that this could not be true for my wife, who received daily letters from me, had shown this correspondence to Joseph Linton – a dear friend and a senior official of the Federation and the Jewish Agency – who had in turn conveyed their contents to these organisations. The reaction from the participants of this meeting left me not just in a state of bewilderment, but deeply incensed at such apparent indifference.

On reflection, however, I asked myself whether I had

misjudged them. Perhaps what appeared as indifference was merely an outward façade whereas deep down they, too, felt a sense of frustration at their inability to make a positive contribution to the alleviation of the problem. As for the Zionist representatives, they, too, must have been utterly despondent at the Government's refusal to open the gates of Palestine to admit these young people whose cause I had pleaded with the High Commissioner for Refugees.

Following this frustrating meeting I called upon Dr Chaim Weizmann to convey to him the hopes and wishes of the young people in Belsen. I was confident that this giant of Jewry who had wielded such influence in the past, could further their cause. But as I spoke to him and described the situation which faced us in Belsen, I saw him visibly shrinking in his chair. Turning to me with a face wracked with pain he said, 'Once I went to the Foreign Office through the front door, now I have to go to the back door like a schnorrer.' What a devastating admission from the man who had been the acknowledged spokesman of world Jewry that the doors of Palestine were barred and bolted and the suffering of Jewry seemed to have made little or no impression on the governments whose armies had liberated the camps.

Were the Jews of Europe, after all, expendable as far as the powers-that-be were concerned?

9

ON THE EXPIRY of my so-called 'leave', I returned to Belsen. The Jewish Relief Team sent by the Jewish Committee for Relief Abroad had settled in well and was doing an excellent job. They were tackling the situation with genuine devotion. They had established a school for the young children and although hampered by lack of materials, were making a decisive impact. In due course they were to create facilities for some of the older generation by introducing courses in occupational therapy.

The Central Jewish Committee under Yossel's leadership was intensifying its activities and it was encouraging to learn that its ranks had been enhanced by the arrival of Rabbi Dr Herman Helfgott, a former chaplain to the Yugoslav army who, on release from captivity, had made his way to Belsen and thrown himself wholeheartedly into the work of the Committee. He was a handsome young man with a striking personality and a beautiful singing voice. He enjoyed great popularity and made a distinctive contribution to the work of the Committee and the maintenance of the morale of the inmates.

As for relations with the Military Government Detachment in charge of the camp it soon became painfully obvious that the Commandant was totally incapable of appreciating the character of the inmates or their reaction to their plight. An incident occurred which reflects this all too clearly and, were it not painful to the inmates concerned, could be regarded as humorous.

The women in the camp were naturally anxious to improve their appearance, and wished to assert their femininity. Some of them, with great ingenuity, cut up army blankets from which they managed to make simple dresses. When the dresses were worn, the letters W.D. were clearly visible. The women were unaware that these letters stood for 'War Department'. They thought that the initials were merely part of the fabric. When this was drawn to the attention of the Commandant he fumed, 'They are misusing military property.' It took a considerable effort to placate this man who had issued an order that the dresses must be confiscated. I explained to him what it meant for the women to have a dress which made them feel they were human again. This imposed quite a strain on an officer who was accustomed to live by a strict book of rules in which an appeal to humanitarian considerations finds no place.

This incident was, in some measure, related to the whole question of relief supplies sent to the camp. As a result of my appeal for clothing when I was in London, a batch of assorted goods had been dispatched to the Central Committee. Alas, some of the contents were disgraceful and beggared description. To my horror I saw them displayed by the Central Committee under an ignominiously worded placard which read '*Englische Relief*'. I was terribly ashamed. It was far from easy to convince my friends on the Committee that clothing and other basic requirements were in short supply in England and that the population had to endure severe rationing of all commodities. But as far as they were concerned this was not included in their calculations.

This pathetic incident contrasted sharply with the behaviour and reaction of other people. On one of my return calls at Army Headquarters I was asked by the officers in the Mess to describe to them the current situation in Belsen since none of them had seen the camp in the course of their military duties. Avoiding the gory details of the diseases with which the medical teams had to contend, I spoke of the after-effects following recovery and the return to a fairly decent state of health. I laid special stress on the needs of the women who were beginning to feel the re-awakening of their femininity after long periods of privation, and I suggested that a valuable contribution to their progress could be made if they were supplied with needles and cotton, wool and knitting needles, face powder and lipstick, hair brushes and combs, all of which would help to bolster their morale.

A young officer, Captain Cartwright, who was present was so impressed with this suggestion that he wrote an impassioned letter to his family in Preston, Lancashire, who in turn sent a copy of his letter to the local press. The result was phenomenal. Within a few weeks a batch of supplies of just these very articles arrived. Attached to each item was a brief message stating that it came from a well-wisher who hoped that the recipient would enjoy it and would soon be restored to good health and reunited with loved ones.

On 10 June I received this letter from Mr Cecil Tragen of Preston:

> I imagine that Captain Cartwright will have informed you of the methods I am using to try to get essential comforts for the released inmates of Belsen.
>
> I am delighted to say that the response has been very good indeed. My wife, Mrs Cartwright, and I have been almost overwhelmed with gifts, many of which must have been a real sacrifice to the donors, especially people in quite humble circumstances. Humanity is still a life force in the world.
>
> Already we have dispatched six parcels and four more will be sent tomorrow. (I am including in this total parcels forwarded by Mrs Cartwright, in addition to those sent by my wife and me.) I hope that the articles will be useful – they include soap, toothpaste, tooth brushes, shaving cream, cosmetics, buttons, razor blades, mirrors, combs etc. etc.

Wherever possible, I have written personal letters of thanks to the donors, but in many cases they were delivered anonymously. I propose, therefore, to write a letter to the local newspaper thanking all those who have provided gifts, when the supply begins to fall off. It is still quite strong and I hope that we will be able to send more parcels during the course of the next week. I would appreciate a letter of thanks from you which I could get inserted in the newspaper in the one which I will send.

Incidentally, I should be glad to know if any parcels have been sent direct to you from people in the Preston district, apart from those which have come through me or Mrs Cartwright. If you have received any such parcels, would it be too much to let me have details of the contents? I am compiling an inventory of all the goods we send and in this way we could get a composite list for record and possible publication purposes.

Captain Cartwright tells me that you have an immense task and he expressed profound admiration for your selfless devotion to duty. May God assist you and lighten your burden. Please don't hesitate to let me know if I can be of possible help to you.

P.S. There was one gift I did not send – The 'Emphasised Gospel of St. John' which has a 'Decision Form' at the back for completion with the name and address of the reader. The Form commences . . . 'Being convinced that I am a sinner . . .' I did not think that such a gift would be gratefully appreciated!

Words are inadequate to describe the impression which such a touching gesture had on all those who received these small, but useful, articles. In some measure it helped to restore faith in humanity and on 13 June I replied to Mr Tragen:

. . . I just cannot find words to express my deep gratitude for all that you and your friends are doing to help those poor unfortunates in the concentration camps. Inadequate though it is, I have tried to convey my appreciation in the enclosed letter which you may send to the local press if you think it is suitable.

Capt. Cartwright who is a brother officer in my mess showed me the extract of the press cutting in which you appealed on my behalf for gifts and comforts. I just did not believe my eyes and now that the stuff is rolling in, I realise that after all there is a basic call of humanity which does not go unanswered.
The following is a list of goods received independently:

Cocoa 2 tins	Coffee 1 tin	Mirrors 4
Shaving soap 12	Toothpaste 18	Toothbrushes 12
Razor blades 10	Face cream 3	Toilet soap 12

I realise all too well that articles of this nature are difficult to obtain and all the greater and deeper is my sense of appreciation.

I wrote the following letter to the Editor of the local paper:

The columns of your journal recently published an appeal to readers to contribute comforts for those who have been victims of Nazi bestiality. May I, therefore, turn to your columns to convey my thanks to all those who have so kindly and generously responded to this appeal.

Thank God the call of basic humanity does not go unanswered. From the depths of degradation and despair these poor victims cry out loud for aid and we have taken it upon ourselves to echo that call. These poor people have been degraded and dehumanised. The Nazis in their cruelty and sadism broke them in mind and body. We found thousands of men, women and children in Belsen who were denied the right to live. They suffered horrors and torture which are indescribable. I once called this camp 'Death's Holiday Camp'. 23,000 people have been buried by us since the camp was liberated. 13,000 died within the first few weeks. They were beyond human aid. Now the forces of liberation are trying to repair the damage to their minds and bodies. We are trying to re-instate them into society and to assure them that they are precious in the sight of God and man.

Through the medium of the gifts I have received we can convey to them that they are not forgotten and that there is a vast number of kind and thoughtful people who feel with them in their suffering.

I cannot convey adequate thanks to all those kind people who have responded to our appeal. There are no words adequate for the occasion. I would only ask those who have given to know that within the camps the recipients will bless their name and long remember that in England's fair shores many still live for whom the love of liberty and the pursuit of happiness are a precious boon.

Relieved as I was to see the effect which the gifts from Preston had on their recipients, I was even happier with the result of an appeal which I made to my brother-in-law, Ben Landau, to help remove the reproach of the *'Englische Relief'*. He energetically undertook to collect articles of clothing of good quality and other comforts from his own community and from business associates. These were never exhibited in Belsen, but were distributed and gratefully received. In some measure this helped to restore Anglo-Jewry to favour and augment its reputation.

Another source of supply of 'goodies' for the inmates came as a result of a letter which I addressed to the troops:

> . . . You may find groups of Jews in the areas in which you are serving. Contact them in our name and give them comfort. Collect their names and first names, the date of their birth and place of origin and send me the information. This is invaluable in that thereby we may help to trace their families. Would you like to make some material contribution too? The men need just those things which you would need in the army. Cigarettes, sweets, chocolates, toothbrushes and toothpaste . . . I shall be happy to deliver [contributions] to the people who need it so much . . .

10

WITH THE PASSAGE of time particular attention had to be directed to the relations between the various organisations involved in the Displaced Persons' problems, the status of the inmates of the camps and especially the complex issues of the Jewish elements.

In order to investigate the problem in depth, a meeting was held on 9 July at Bad Oeynhausen, the Headquarters of 21 Army Group, at which Major Kitson of Military Government presided. In attendance were Colonel Macpherson of UNRRA, Colonel Agnew of the British Red Cross, Mr Jacob Trobe of the American Joint Distribution Committee, Mr Leonard Cohen of the Jewish Committee for Relief Abroad, Mr Shalom Markovitch, leader of a Jewish Relief Unit, and myself.

Consideration was given to some form of co-operation between the British and the Americans in the relief operation, but it soon became evident that each had to work independently as the auspices under which they operated varied so considerably.

The need to facilitate the bringing together of families was deemed essential and should be given priority. To this end it was agreed that complete registration of all D.P.s should be undertaken. UNRRA assumed this immense task and proposed the establishment of a central information control for the whole of the British Zone. Belsen had already created its own central Jewish search bureau and the Central Jewish Committee had published its own list of survivors under the title *She'erit Ha'Pletah*.

I raised two vital matters regarding the future of Jewish D.P.s, their status and possible re-location. Once again I put forward the case for the segregation of Jewish D.P.s and locating them in villages where provision could be made for their special needs. This proposal was strongly supported by Mr Trobe and Mr Cohen who were requested to submit their arguments in writing. This they did and the following is the text of their memorandum:

REGROUPING OF JEWISH DISPLACED PERSONS   Most of the D.P.s from Western Europe have now been evacuated to their former homes, and those from Central Europe who wish to return to their homes are being enabled to do so. Amongst those who will be left are the Jewish D.P.s from Poland, Hungary and other Eastern European countries. This group is unwilling to return to its countries of origin because for a long period of years they have been subjected to severe economic and social discrimination as Jews. Further, in the case of the specific Polish issue, the vast majority, if not all Jewish D.P.s from Poland, are unwilling to return to Poland under any political regime. With extermination of over six millions of Jews in Central Europe, it is probable that these D.P.s are the only surviving members of their families. As a result of Nazi tyranny, Eastern Europe has been converted into a mass graveyard of Jewish victims.

SEGREGATION OF JEWISH D.P.S   It is submitted that a distinct case should be made in relation to Jewish D.P.s now found within the British Zone of Occupation, and which would also be applicable throughout Germany. It is requested that consideration should be given to the establishment of Jewish villages, where these non-repatriable Jewish D.P.s could be housed until arrangements can be made for their resettlement.

From all observations of the relations existing between the Jewish and non-Jewish groups from Eastern Europe, it is evident that it is psychologically unhealthy to maintain a policy of segregation based only upon nationality.

PRESENT SITUATION   The Jewish D.P.s were deported on racial grounds, and almost all of them have been for many years in concentration camps under the worst possible conditions, and are consequently in a lower state of physical and mental health than the other D.P.s. At the moment segregation in relation to D.P.s calculated on the basis of nationality, has proved unsatisfactory in relation to the specific problems of Jews from Eastern Europe. It has been proved that even within the camps, Jews have suffered from discrimination and victimisation at the hands of non-Jewish D.P.s.

SUGGESTED SEGREGATION   It is submitted that such Jewish D.P.s should be concentrated. In order to facilitate the efforts of relief workers and Military Government to rehabilitate these D.P.s, it is further submitted that such concentration should take the form of Jewish villages, where they can begin to live a normal life and prepare themselves for the responsibilities of life in the countries of ultimate settlement.

It is estimated that the total possible number of such Jewish D.P.s will not exceed 20,000 within the British Zone of Occupation. Working on the precedent in the creation of Polish villages which were set up some time ago, the whole problem of Jewish villages could be resolved by the requisition of four villages, each containing 5,000 D.P.s.

To the observer entering Germany, it seems incredible that the victims of Nazi Germany are still subjected to the rigours and hardships of D.P. camps, when in their immediate proximity, their sometime oppressors and persecutors remain at ease and comfort.

The second issue I raised concerned the status of those D.P.s who were former German nationals living both inside and outside D.P. camps. These, I had reason to believe, were being treated on the same basis as other German civilians. In view of the hardship and suffering which they had undergone in the concentration camps and of their consequent physical and mental condition, they surely deserved special consideration. The chairman assured me that this matter would be taken up.

The assurances given to us at this meeting offered some measure of comfort and we felt that we had made some impression. Unfortunately the outcome was far from satisfactory. Our plea for the creation of Jewish villages produced no positive response. As for my submission on behalf of the German Jews – that, too, failed to gain acceptance. As nothing tangible emerged I addressed a special plea to the Director of Civil Affairs Branch of Military Government making special reference to the German Jews who had returned to the cities, and in particular to Berlin where I had gained an insight into the plight of the returnees. His reply, which I reproduce, left much to be desired:

SUBJECT – GERMAN JEWS

1. The policy which is being adopted is that emphasis should be placed on a Jew's political nationality rather than on his race or religious persuasion. Preferential treatment of Jews would be unfair to the many non-Jews in Germany who have suffered on account of their activities in the cause of the Allies. Furthermore segregation and special treatment of the Jews would be likely to cause anti-Jewish feeling which it is particularly desirable to avoid.

2. Jews in the D.P. camps are treated in the same way as D.P.s of other nationalities. German Jews found in concentration camps are treated in the same way as other inmates. When restored to health they are, if they wish, permitted to return to their homes in Germany. After their return home these Jews are treated as other Germans. It would be administratively impracticable and also against the interest of the Jews themselves to do otherwise.

I was obviously not in a position to question the validity of the arguments contained in this letter. To compare the suffering of

Jews with those non-Jews who, it was alleged, were active on the side of the Allies, was highly questionable. The 'fair play' attitude struck me as totally miscast barely three months after the end of hostilities.

I could, however, appreciate the difficulties which the civilian population presented, particularly in Berlin where the situation there was chaotic – with the administration divided between the British, Russians and Americans there was little hope that the Jews would enjoy special consideration. The only exception in relation to Jewish civilians which the authorities had to concede, was the non-application of the no-fraternisation order which had been in force since the early days of the collapse of the German Army. It was readily appreciated that this could not apply to any relief work undertaken on behalf of Jewish civilians.

11

THE ATMOSPHERE INSIDE Belsen never remained calm for long. Eruptions were liable to break out with a minimum of provocation, or as a result of misunderstanding. Clashes of personality contributed to tensions within the administration of the camp. To act as mediator between the inmates and the authorities was invariably fraught with difficulties. Thus it again fell to my lot to convey a series of complaints to H.Q. Military Government made by the Central Committee regarding the attitude of the Commandant to its Chairman and the Jewish inmates:

1. The Commandant refused to receive the Chairman who was the acknowledged spokesman of the Jews in the camp.
2. Displaced Persons arriving at Belsen from other camps in the hope of being reunited with their families were refused admittance. (It was a recognised fact that D.P.s were constantly on the move throughout the Zone hoping that by some chance they might find members of their families.)
3. The administration of all former Polish citizens was being passed to the Polish Committee contrary to the wishes of the Polish Jews.
4. The vehicle registered at Belsen and allocated for the use of the Chairman of the Jewish Committee had been withdrawn,

thus depriving him of the opportunity to make contact with Jews in other D.P. centres.

5. The Chairman had been threatened with arrest.

6. The general feeling in the camp was that the Commandant was conducting an intrigue against the Jewish D.P.s in making promises of goodwill towards them and then revoking them without provocation.

As the submission of these complaints could be interpreted as an adverse report on an army officer, I was duty bound, in accordance with military procedure, to send the Commandant a copy of my communication. A copy of his response to these accusations, the contents of which were far from satisfactory, was duly sent to me. It was blatantly obvious that the friction which existed between Yossel and the Commandant was exacerbated by the visit of representatives of the American Joint Distribution Committee. The Commandant preferred to deal with them rather than with Yossel who refused to recognise them as spokesmen for the Jewish inmates of Belsen. In this he was more than justified, but he spoke only Yiddish and required the services of an interpreter, and the Joint and the Commandant had, at least, a common language. As for the refusal of admittance to the wandering D.P.s, this was categorically denied. Whilst this might have occurred in individual cases, by and large the complaint was unjustified. It was, however, submitted that it was beyond the capacity of the administration to control the numbers who entered the camp because of the constant movements of inmates in and out of the camp. This imposed a severe burden on the administration, particularly in regard to housing and feeding the inmates. As for the withdrawal of the vehicle allocated to the Chairman, this too, was admitted, but its misuse was not defined.

The Commandant also accepted that he had threatened Yossel with arrest and gave the reason that Yossel refused to limit his activities to Belsen and regularly defied orders given to him by British officers. This came as no surprise to me knowing

Yossel's temperament. He was not the type to be subjected to an imposed discipline. This was how he had managed to survive. Belsen was merely an extension of previous incarcerations.

As Chairman of the Central Committee he regarded himself as the spokesman for all Jewish D.P.s in the British Zone and Belsen was the centre from which would radiate all the influences which would affect the welfare of all Jewish D.P.s. This was the primary cause of conflict with the authorities who, many of the D.P.s felt, were unsympathetic, hence the belief that the Commandant was conducting a vendetta against Yossel and his Committee. This was clearly a case of the 'irresistible force meeting an immovable object'.

The power which Yossel wielded over his fellow inmates was immense and his organising ability was generally acknowledged. It was largely due to him that the internal conditions in the camp were enhanced and life made more bearable. He was responsible for encouraging those who possessed artistic talent to use it for the benefit of their fellow inmates. Thus a theatrical group was established which gave regular performances which helped to relieve the tedium and the listlessness which was so prevalent in the camp. The fiery, uncompromising Yossel was, above all else, a man who was politically motivated. He was convinced that unless Jews were regarded as a distinct entity and received the consideration due to them because of their suffering, their case would go by default and they would be submerged into the morass of the entire D.P. situation. His conviction was given eloquent expression on the historic occasion when Mr Earl Harrison, representing the President of the United States of America, visited Belsen. This imposing personality, equipped as he was with such representative powers, could not deflect Yossel from addressing him in forthright terms.

Speaking in Yiddish, as was his wont, which was then translated, Yossel presented a picture of Jewish suffering which should have moved the most stony-hearted, but although the emotion with which it was delivered was most impressive, alas much of its power was lost in translation. It was then my turn to speak of the plight of the Jewish D.P.s. I well recall my own impassioned remarks addressed particularly to the role which the free nations played in the early days of the Nazi regime when, by barring entry to refugees, they had directly contributed to the enormous losses that Jewry had sustained. I urged Mr Harrison to use his high office to facilitate the emigration of Jewish D.P.s to the countries of their choice and especially to Palestine. If he failed to do so he would denigrate the validity of those immortal words composed by Emma Lazarus which so aptly described the Jews concentrated in Bergen-Belsen and which are inscribed on the base of the Statue of Liberty.

> Give me your tired, your poor
> Your huddled masses yearning to breathe free.
> The wretched refuse of your teeming shore.
> Send these, the homeless, tempest-tossed to me.
> I lift my lamp beside the Golden door.

What impact this meeting and the stirring speeches to which he listened had on Earl Harrison I cannot now recall. He was moved I know, but whether any report which he may have passed to the American President had any effect remains doubtful. One thing is certain, the visit and the contents of that meeting with so eminent a visitor gave a distinct boost to the morale of the Central Committee who felt that they had been the true spokesmen of all the Jewish D.P.s.

Another boost to the flagging spirits of the Belsen D.P.s came from a visit by representatives of the Jewish Brigade which was then stationed in Antwerp. After involvement in the final stages of the war in Italy, the Brigade moved northwards believing that it would participate in the final defeat of the German army on German soil. The military authorities, however, denied them this privilege. They feared the possible consequences of an all-Jewish military formation coming into contact with German civilians which might lead to uncontrolled acts of revenge. The Brigade was, therefore, forced to remain outside German territory and was left to 'cool off' in Belgium until the cessation of hostilities.

Nor were members of the Brigade to receive official permission to make contact with the inmates of Belsen, but this did not deter them from paying illicit visits to the camp and to offer encouragement to the inmates. The dominant incentive of these visits was the search for missing relatives. The Brigade was a Palestinian unit and since nearly every Palestinian Jew had a relative, however distant, who originated from Central or Eastern Europe, the hope remained constant that members of the family would ultimately be re-united.

As a direct outcome of such visits to Belsen and to other camps with which the Brigade made contact on its trek though Europe, the Welfare Department of the Brigade produced a detailed memorandum (see Appendix A, p. 113) on the problems of the D.P.s and the condition in the camps, offering suggestions for the amelioration of their plight and their ultimate rehabilitation.

It was evident that such a memorandum composed by a group of men who were supremely conscious of their own status as Palestinians, and had experienced the exigencies of military service, many of them in the Haganah, should present a positive solution to so complex a problem. Hence their proposal – now all too familiar – that special Jewish displaced persons' camps be established where the peculiar needs of Jews could be provided and cultural, educational and occupational facilities be made available which would help to equip them for their future life. These special camps would serve as a welcoming temporary home for those Jews who were wandering from country to country in search of surviving members of their families and who were living on what they could obtain from the local population, often by illegal means.

As for the ultimate solution, the proposal was predictable. It stated that Jews be allowed to emigrate to Palestine.

Typical of the spirit of resistance to adverse conditions was the audacious act of one youngster in Belsen. He approached me one day to say that he was leaving the camp and would make his way across Europe to his native town in Poland. There he planned to search for any relatives or friends who might have survived and to see whether anything was left of his family's property. All my efforts to dissuade him from such a perilous undertaking were of no avail. He was determined to go and off he went.

Some weeks later he returned – he had found no relatives nor the home in which he and his family once lived. What he had discovered, however, was the best route across Europe which could be used for ultimate Aliyah to Palestine. He called it the 'Underground Route' which the British authorities would never uncover. How right he was. This was the route adopted by so many brave and determined young people who, with the help of the Jewish Agency and the Haganah, would reach their desired destination.

Whilst it was hoped that all surviving children would enjoy a new life and recover from the traumas of their recent experiences in Palestine, negotiations were in progress between refugee organisations and the Home Office for permission to be granted for the admission of a limited number to the United Kingdom.

Sir Alexander Maxwell wrote to Otto Schiff on 1 June:

> The Home Secretary has now had an opportunity of considering the suggestion which you made that the Refugee Organisations should be allowed to bring to this country up to 1,000 children from concentration camps in Germany on the understanding that the voluntary organisations would make themselves responsible for the care of the children while here and for their ultimate disposal. The Home Secretary has asked me to let you know that he is prepared to agree to this proposal

subject, of course, to proper arrangements being made for the
medical examination of the children before they are brought
here, for their transport and for their accommodation in this
country. It is understood that while most of the children in
these camps are probably Jewish, there will be no attempt to
limit the selection of children to be brought into this country to
Jewish children. Miss Bracey told me that the Friends
Organisation will be willing to share in the scheme and take
responsibility for non-Jewish children.

In conversation with me, when using the word 'children',
you did not mention any age, but the Home Secretary said he
assumed that you meant children under 14 years of age and,
though I don't think it is necessary to lay down hard and fast
rules excluding boys or girls a little over this age, yet I think
generally speaking the children selected for admission to this
country should be under 14.

It must, of course, be understood that this is an exceptional
arrangement made for dealing with the specially pitiful
condition of children found in concentration camps, and must
not be taken as a precedent for requests to bring to this country
other children or young persons, or older persons, who are in a
distressed condition on the Continent.

Otto Schiff, writing on behalf of the Jewish Refugees'
Committee, sent me a copy of the letter from the Home Office
together with a personal letter:

... Of the 1,000 it is estimated that a small percentage will be
non-Jewish, as the Friends Committee is also interested in the
matter and it was on this understanding that the necessary
permission was given by the Home Office.

The question now is how to select these children and I feel
that before taking any steps I would like to have your advice
and estimate of the number of children whom you could select
from the area covered by you. Children in Lingen would be
eligible, but not children who are living in towns or villages and
are not in the camps.

Ultimately, no doubt, we shall have to make arrangements

for the emigration of the children, but this will not come into question for some considerable time.

We are getting into touch with the War Office in connection with transport etc., but I think that if you in your Zone and the American Joint – with whom I am communicating on similar lines – in the American Zone could help us in the selection of the children that would be most satisfactory.

I should however, be glad to have your immediate reply as I am anxious not to waste time in getting the children over. Try as far as possible to concentrate on children under the age of 14 years. I do not think we should take children who are with any relative in a camp, unless it is a very distant one. Splitting up of families does not seem to be wise at the present juncture, as it may be very difficult to reunite them.

He wrote to me again on 14 June:

... I wonder if you could arrange, on our behalf, to have a nominal roll made of the children who you think could be brought over from your area to this country. I think we should be allowed to take them up to the age of about 16 years. The kind of information we should need on such a roll would be name, present whereabouts, date of birth or age, sex and any further details which you consider relevant. I am afraid that this is putting still more work on you but I am hoping that you can get one or other of the relief workers or chaplains in each camp, to do this and I feel that you and they will not mind undertaking so constructive a task.

I am looking forward to seeing you next week and I am calling a meeting for Tuesday June 26th at 4 p.m. I will let you know where it is to be. It will be representative of all the organisations concerned with the problems you have at heart. I do hope that this will suit you, but as I wanted to be sure of getting all the really useful people together, I did not dare leave it until I could obtain your confirmation, and have fixed this up. In any case I hope to see you soon after your arrival.

I heard again from the Jewish Refugees' Committee on 20 August:

It was indeed a great joy for us to receive the messages and we will certainly do our utmost to facilitate their reaching their destination as speedily as possible and bring joy to relatives from whom they have been cut off for so many years.

I was most interested to learn that you have been in Berlin and certainly hope that with your phenomenal vigour you have arranged for complete lists to be forwarded to us as speedily as possible.

I am sure that you will be glad to hear that the first group of children to be admitted to this country arrived on Tuesday night. They were 300 orphans from Theresienstadt, an extraordinary good bunch of children in a fairly good state of health. Now that we have really started in on this scheme, we do hope that it will not be long before we can absorb further hundreds from the British and American Zones. I am afraid, however, that a delay is inevitable as the question of finding accommodation, staff etc., is as grim as ever over here.

It was good news to hear that there is peace at last, but the problems of Europe are hardly nearer solution.

In spite of protracted negotiations Belsen children were not sent to England. In October 1945 the Jewish Committee reached the following conclusion:

1. That it cannot agree to the removal of children to England.
2. That it cannot permit children who were with us in the ghettos and concentration camps to be moved from Galut to Galut. They must stay where they are until their Aliyah.
3. It demands that the first available Aliyah certificates be allocated to children so that they may leave the camps as soon as possible.

The committee maintained this resolve. In April 1946, 200 certificates were granted to the children of Belsen. They, together with many hundreds of children collected from various parts of Germany set sail from Marseilles accompanied by Hadassah Bimko. On their arrival in Haifa they were allocated to various Kibbutzim.

12

MEANWHILE NEW PROBLEMS were developing among the inmates of Belsen which should have been foreseen. Men and women were regaining their physical strength and the natural desire to live a normal life was awakened. They wished to marry and produce children, not just to satisfy their newly revived sexuality, but to prove to the world that the Jewish people was indestructible and that the vast gap created by Nazi enormity could be filled.

Sympathetic as I naturally was and eager to assist them by performing religious marriages, I pleaded for a minimum delay until I could obtain the necessary authority from the London Beth Din. I wrote to London drawing attention to the fact that applicants for marriage were convinced that there was no impediment to such ceremonies. Those who had been previously married were certain that their former spouses were no longer alive – many had seen them directed to their death.

The response received from the Beth Din filled me with dismay. Under no circumstances were marriages to be performed until a complete list of all survivors had been drawn up: there was always the possibility that somewhere a former wife or husband might have survived their ordeal and therefore a second marriage would be bigamous.

How little did the Beth Din understand the situation. D.P.s

were wandering over the face of Europe, so how could a comprehensive list be compiled? Must these survivors be doomed to an indefinite period of celibacy? It was unnatural and unthinkable. Even Rabbi Baumgarten, the representative of Orthodoxy in Belsen, realised this and knowing that with or without formal marriage some inmates would cohabit, he succeeded in prevailing upon the Army engineers to assist in building a Mikvah under his supervision. Thus equipped with the religious pre-requisite, he issued an order that no marriages could be performed until the Mikvah was completed. How many brides availed themselves of this amenity I was unable to ascertain. I do know that many inmates treated the Rabbi's instruction with disdain and those who were convinced sceptics virtually laughed him out of court.

A couple came to see me and handed me a piece of paper on which was written in Yiddish 'I ... son of ... take ... daughter of ... as my wife' to which was appended the signatures of two witnesses. This was an acceptable document whose legality could not be questioned. Before, however, I assured them of its acceptability, I questioned them as to their former status. The answers they gave left me in no doubt that this was not an unusual case. They had both been in Auschwitz, as the tattoos on their arms testified: 'I was directed to the right and my wife to the left,' he stated. That his wife had gone straight to her death, there was no doubt. I was convinced that even the most stringent Beth Din would have to accept that as adequate testimony.

Whilst the question of marriages might be high on the agenda, a much more serious issue was developing to which little or no attention was directed. I confess that I knew nothing of it until a Jewish medical officer attached to the camp submitted a memorandum to the Commandant, a copy of which he passed to me. I realised that we were faced with a moral issue which would have to be tackled with the utmost sensitivity.

There is a very serious problem in the camp which must be dealt with immediately. There are a great number – estimated at several hundred – of single women and young girls who are pregnant.

One can appreciate how such a situation has arisen. After their terrible and ghastly experiences, losing their parents, husbands and children, existing for years without human affection, without friends and advisers, they would not know how to react to the first person who showed them a little sympathy.

Whilst it is easily understandable and humanly excusable to account for their present state, nevertheless they find themselves in a dreadful social and moral dilemma full of tragic consequences. Their situation undermines all their hopes for a better and happier future. They fear that the child they are bearing will make it impossible to return to a normal life.

Ashamed, desperate, helpless, their one desire is to get rid of their pregnancy. Unfortunately, to accomplish these abortions the majority are consulting 'quacks'. In so doing these young women are exposing themselves to the very gravest of dangers for both their health and physical existence and for the moral basis of their spiritual life. Others consult the camp doctors and ask to be relieved of their pregnancy. In spite of our desire to help them in the best manner possible, we are convinced that we have to refuse their requests.

It is the duty of the doctor to make himself adviser to these women meeting them with the greatest compassion. He must afford them all possible moral assistance and re-animate in them the sense of respect for human life. Not least important is to instil in the expectant mother a sense of responsibility and a feeling of dignity for the new life she is about to create. But this cannot be done under the conditions in which they are at present living.

It is an urgent and irrefutable duty of society to help these women by establishing for them a house where they can pass the months of their pregnancy in the best moral and material conditions. This home should be distant from the camp and offer its inmates an atmosphere of sympathy and understanding. It is not intended that these women should be idle, but a

programme of manual work, professional training, child care
and general instruction should be undertaken.

The home should be able to accommodate at least 200
people and so arranged that members of different faiths can live
in accordance with their religious traditions. This spiritual factor
is essential for their rehabilitation. Such a plan would reduce the
number of abortions which are being performed with all the
obvious grievous physical and moral dangers resulting from
them, and would create a sense of acceptance of the child. For
many the trauma of finding themselves pregnant will eventually
become a reason for renewed hope for the future.

To my great regret I was not in the position to follow up
this proposition as I was called back to London for a spell of
temporary duty and by the time I returned to Belsen the whole
scheme went by default. Nor was I able to discover the exact
number of women who had to face this dilemma, for in the
meantime we were faced with another grave issue which
demanded our attention.

It was indeed most unfortunate that at such a critical time we
should have to call into question the activities of the Chief
Rabbi's Religious Emergency Council which was directed by
Rabbi Dr Solomon Schonfeld, the Chief Rabbi's son-in-law.
The purpose of this Council was to provide religious amenities
and where necessary stimulate or revive religious activities. To
his credit it must be stated that Schonfeld was dedicated to the
task of saving Jewish children. The means he employed were
sometimes questionable, but he did succeed in bringing hundreds of children to England and to him they owe their lives
and their future careers. But during this period, critical as it was
for the Jews in Belsen, every assistance that could be rendered
by well-wishers abroad was desperately needed. Schonfeld
however, insisted on sending parcels only to what he called the
'Kehillah' or Gemeinde, by which he meant the religious
element, totally disregarding those who did not fit into this

category. As his agent for the distribution of these amenities he nominated Rabbi Vilensky. The choice of this man was most unfortunate for we soon learned that his integrity left much to be desired. Dr Redcliffe Salaman, Chairman of the Jewish Committee for Relief Abroad, reacted by writing to Rabbis Baumgarten and Vilensky:

17 August

On 9th August, Mr. Leonard Cohen and myself were informed by Dr. Schonfeld, in the presence of Dayan Lazarus, that he had instructed you to take abroad certain articles of value to be used for certain purposes which I need not detail here.

This information has greatly distressed the Hon. Officers who wish to dissociate themselves entirely from any such instruction. I have to inform you that the use of such methods in the British Zone of Occupation would be diametrically opposed to their wishes, and they are confident that in the long run, such would react to the detriment of the very people you have gone out to help.

In as much as you are working under the aegis of the Jewish Committee for Relief Abroad, we are responsible for your activities whilst on service, and I must ask you to regard it as an order that, whilst this relationship exists, the instructions given to you by Dr. Schonfeld shall be cancelled and void.

This letter has been submitted to Rabbi Brodie and has his full approval.

The discrimination which Schonfeld showed in favour of what he deemed the religious inmates was roundly condemned by the Central Committee and, in my view, rightly so. In the face of such provocation the Committee issued a statement over the signatures of the Chairman, representatives of the Jewish Committee for Relief Abroad and the American Joint to the effect that all supplies such as books, food, clothing etc. should be addressed to the Committee for fair distribution.

Rabbi Schonfeld disregarded this request and persisted in his own method of distribution. On a subsequent visit to London I attended a meeting held at the Board of Deputies under the chairmanship of its President, Professor Selig Brotetsky, convened for the express purpose of discussing the situation in Belsen. Schonfeld was also present and when the activities of his Council came up for discussion he justified his action by stating that whereas the non-religious elements engaged in 'organising' their required supplies by foraging in the neighbourhood, the religious inmates were engaged in more 'godly' activities. Such blatant nonsense and misrepresentation infuriated me. In my heated response I denied that there was any truth in his observations but more relevant was the fact that since Hitler made no distinction between one Jew and another, what right had we to do so. They were our people whatever their religious viewpoints and we should treat them all as equal victims of a cruel fate. I was heartened to gain the support of the chairman, but Schonfeld, exploiting the name of the Chief Rabbi, was unrepentant.

Vilensky's actions within Belsen enraged many of the inmates, so much so that for a time he was kept under house arrest for his own safety. I wanted him removed from Germany and on 27 September wrote to Dr Salaman:

As is well known, he [Vilensky] together with his two colleagues, were sent across in response to my appeal for chaplains. Military chaplains not being available these civilians were placed at our disposal. At the request of the military I was called in to advise on their allocation to the camps. Vilensky was duly sent to Belsen. Never at any time has he sent me a report on his activities, and when asked to do so some weeks ago, he informed me that he is not responsible to me but had direct access to the highest authorities. Although prepared to overlook this point, I realise now that had I made sufficient demand for such reports much subsequent trouble might have been averted. Never at any time has Dr. Schonfeld led me to believe that these Rabbis serve in an independent capacity.

Since I was informed yesterday by Dr. Schonfeld that these Rabbis were responsible to me for administration, I feel I must now submit an adverse report on Vilensky and ask that you use your kind offices to remove him.

My charges are as follows:

1. He obtained his transport from H.Q. 21 Army Group without consulting me. When asked by the Officer Commanding Military Government at Belsen, he stated that I had obtained the same for him.

2. This officer informed me that Vilensky was posing as the 'plenipotentiary of the Chief Rabbi' and was travelling around the country indulging in 'political activities' – whatever that means.

3. He has neglected his duties at Belsen in that he never visited the hospitals where so many patients are lying in the wards.

4. He has constantly indulged in intrigue against the officially recognised Central Jewish Committee of Belsen.

5. He has stirred up the inmates of Belsen to dissatisfaction, and as a result of inflammatory speeches he was attacked by some of the inmates recently, and was ordered by Mil. Govt. to remain confined to his room.

6. He has distributed 'largesse' to officers and inmates, which can only be interpreted as attempts to bribe people to support him against his opponents.

I think I can sum up the situation by stating that even if these charges are considered of no importance, the very fact that he does not enjoy the confidence of the inmates of Belsen and has enraged them with his provocations, is sufficient to prove his unworthiness to hold so important an office.

I do most earnestly ask you to assist me to restore peace to the camp by removing him from our midst.

Ultimately, Vilensky was removed from Belsen.

There are times when troubles do not come singly to cause aggravation and heartache. Just prior to my London visit the

Senior Staff Chaplain, a Methodist minister, asked me to do him a special favour. He needed a new cassock, he told me, and would I therefore be good enough to enquire at the clerical tailors as to prices, qualities etc. On my return I informed him that there were two qualities of material each requiring a different number of clothing coupons – rationing was severe at that time and coupons were required for almost everything. To my utter amazement, instead of thanking me for the trouble I had taken, his immediate reaction was, 'Of course I should have known better. Your people have cornered the cloth market.' Although he was my superior in rank I could not control my anger. All I could say to this ingrate was, 'You're an ungrateful bastard' and stormed out of his office!

I can truthfully say that this was the only time I was ever confronted by blatant anti-Semitism from an officer in the whole of my military career. That it should have occurred in Germany of all places, added a measure of poignancy to the occasion.

One day, out of the blue, I received a message from an officer in charge of Field Security which said that a cache of unusual documents and artefacts had been uncovered in a village in the province of Hanover and would I go there and report on the contents. Armed with the necessary map reference I located the village and found a small school house. To my astonishment it was like an Aladdin's cave filled with a huge variety of objects. As I proceeded to sort them, I found hundreds of Masonic medallions, several Sifrei Torah in good condition, except for one burnt relic, a number of Schechita knives and several plaques to which were attached the most lurid photographs. These depicted *Stürmer*-like representations of 'hateful' Jews in the act of ritual slaughter each of which was accompanied by such captions as '*So Schachtet der Jude*. The cruel gleam in his eyes clearly evident.' Among this sordid collection I found a booklet entitled *Der Talmud Jude* which was originally written towards the end of the last century by the notorious August Rohling who was involved in a famous libel case with Rabbi Samuel Bloch.

Rohling was a non-Jewish Professor of Hebrew Antiquities at the University of Prague. He issued a scurrilous statement about the attitude of Talmudic Rabbis to non-Jews. Bloch wrote an article in the press accusing him of 'practising falsehood as a profession'. Rohling reacted by suing Bloch for libel, but when the case reached the courts the evidence presented by two learned scholars, Noeldecke and Wunsche, proved that Rohling was totally ignorant of Rabbinical Judaism. When *Der Talmud Jude* first appeared, thousands of copies were disseminated throughout Austria with the aim of stimulating anti-Judaism among the masses. It was just the type of text book which was used by Alfred Rosenberg, Nazi ideologist and minister of occupied territories in the east, from 1941, for his anti-Jewish fulminations.

This assortment of anti-Masonic and anti-Jewish material, and especially the character of the plaques, led me to believe the collection must have once served as an exhibition promoted by the former Gauleiter of Hanover and had been hastily dumped in the school house when the Nazi regime collapsed. Whilst I could make no use of the Masonic material, I gathered together the Jewish objects. I notified the military authorities of my findings, and with their agreement distributed the Sifrei Torah and the Schechita knives to the nascent Jewish communities in the British Zone in the hope that they would help in the revival of Jewish life and activity. The burnt Sefer Torah relic and the exhibition plaques I retained in my personal possession as a painful souvenir of the odious propaganda which had helped to inflame such anti-Jewish hatred during the Nazi regime.

13

THE DISPLACED PERSONS' camp at Kaunitz housed some 400 Hungarian Jews, and there I met a representative of the Hungarian Red Cross who had been sent to arrange for the transportation and repatriation of these nationals. I wrote to the Commander of the 3rd British Infantry Division asking if he would obtain transport to arrange for this repatriation. The best route appeared to be via Pilsen where the Czech authorities would arrange for the onward journey of these D.P.s.

This disappointing reply was dated 24 July:

Nothing has been notified about the repatriation of Hungarians. Any official, ad hoc, plans for the evacuation of Hungarians would almost certainly result in their being turned back at the frontier.

This formation is unable to despatch transport to Czechoslovakia without instruction from 1 Corps District.
It is suggested that the representatives of the Hungarian Red Cross be invited to contact H.Q. 21 Army Group with a view to arranging for the evacuation of these persons officially.

The 'buck' had been passed and no transport was arranged at that time.

Cigarettes were an important commodity in the barter market and the value placed on them could provide necessities. They, and the Hungarian Jews at Kaunitz, also involved me in correspondence with the Kadimah Society (an organisation for young Zionists) in London, who first wrote to me on 13 August 1945:

> We should be greatly obliged if you would inform us how many of the 36,000 cigarettes sent by us have arrived, if possible giving the reference numbers or names which figured on the parcels received by you to enable us to claim the missing parcels, if any, through the firms with whom we had placed our orders.
>
> It seems to us that there must be considerable delay in the delivery of the cigarettes as Rev. Elton, who has just returned to this country, informed us that Dr. Andor Klein complained to him recently that the Hungarians have received only very few cigarettes and that at the time of their meeting he had practically no cigarettes to distribute. This fact is rather disappointing for us as we have been doing our best to provide our Hungarian brethren there with a continuous supply of cigarettes.
>
> Would you also be kind enough to inform us which other parcels have reached you for the benefit of the Hungarian Jews in the camp as we do not think it to be advisable to send parcels unless at least a greater part of them arrives at their destination.

> 17 August 1945

> We would be greatly obliged if you could see your way to helping us in the following matter.
>
> Rev. M. Elton has just received a letter dated 17th July from one of his cousins who is interned in the camp in Kaunitz, informing him that three Hungarian delegates visited the camp and told them that within two or three weeks they will be returned to Hungary. She complains in her letter that they are in bad need of clothing, food and cigarettes.
>
> We would ask you to be kind enough to state if the people in Kaunitz have been returned to Hungary and in case they are still there, to help them with the most necessary things, mainly

cigarettes, and we shall make up for it in the shortest possible time.

I sent an exasperated reply to both letters on 22 August:

I would like to inform you that there is no means of checking every parcel which arrives at this office. I have a staff comprising one clerk. You must realise what this means in terms of military and civilian work and how we are overloaded. Parcels arrive in the name of many people, especially cigarettes ex factories. We cannot possibly keep account of each name. Neither is it possible to know whether the names which appear on the parcels refer to organisations or private persons. I would ask you, therefore, to be good enough and accept my thanks in toto for all that has been sent and to be assured that the parcels are dispatched to their destinations as they arrive here.

Further I would like to inform you that I do not specialise in any specific nationality. All parcels are pooled. I send some to Belsen to be distributed by the Jewish Committee and the Relief Team. I have also given cigarettes and parcels to Mr. Elton specifying that the same should be distributed in his area. We dare not differentiate. If you desire to assist only Hungarians, I must refrain from participating, since all have suffered equally and deserve an equal share of assistance. As for Dr. Klein's complaint. Since he is a member of the Jewish Committee of Belsen it is his duty to be active in helping all his fellow Jews and should be aware of the method of distributing relief.

With regard to Kaunitz I can only pass on the information to the Relief Organisation and ask them to look into the matter. In fact the Kaunitz camp is the best in the whole British Zone and there is certainly no reason for them to complain of shortages. They are living comfortably and are being 'petted' by the military authorities. Alas there are some who constantly complain and are never satisfied.

14

As THE MONTHS passed following the cessation of hostilities, the army of occupation became engaged in routine duties. Some form of stimulation to counteract the inevitable consequences of idleness was needed. I discussed this problem with Colonel Backhouse, an eminent lawyer, and together we devised a series of debates when he and I would appear before the troops in various units to discuss the subject of German guilt and the extent to which the general public was aware of the implications of the Holocaust – although at that time this term was unknown.

I presented the case for the prosecution. I claimed that no German could plead ignorance. The intense anti-Jewish propaganda which was the major theme of Hitler's ravings and the dissemination of the *Stürmer* with its lurid caricatures of the demonic Jew could not have passed unnoticed. More significant was the removal of Jewish children from schools, and adults from professions; the prohibition of Jewish appearances in public places, the imposition of the yellow star and the mass deportations leading to so much Jewish property passing into non-Jewish hands. This must have made an impact on the civilian population.

In his response, Backhouse argued that whilst he agreed that the population must have been indoctrinated in Jew hatred, it did not imply that the consequences of the Final Solution were generally known. Jews were transported to the east where the death factories were installed but the population was kept in ignorance of the methods employed there to exterminate Jews. They were constantly informed that these transportations were designed to enhance the labour force for the benefit of the Reich and the war effort.

'What of Belsen?' I argued. 'Did the local population not see the arrival of thousands of haggard and wretched victims, and when the area was isolated because of the typhus epidemic, they must have realised that something dreadful was happening.' He replied, 'How many back in England who live in the vicinity of the state prisons know what goes on behind the walls of those institutions?'

To what extent these public debates made an impact on the troops, it was impossible to gauge at the time. I was convinced that we had given them food for thought, but as time went by I had reason to believe that there was still cause for disquiet. We were now faced with the insidious effects of fraternisation between the troops and the civilian German population.

Shortly after the collapse and defeat of the German Army an order was issued by the Commander in Chief of Allied Forces to the effect that fraternisation with the German civilian population was strictly forbidden. The Americans were the first to relax these restrictions and the British soon followed their example. While listening to the radio on 11 July I heard that this relaxation was to be formalised. That evening I wrote to my wife.

It is seven p.m. and my table has just been cleared at long last. Several interruptions with people coming in to see me but the mess is removed and I feel a strange sense of relief that no-one is waiting for a reply any longer. And the house is clean too and so is my office. I now have two German women coming in each day to clean the house down. They started this morning and worked well. They are thorough, damn them, and I am certain that many Englishmen will look on and admire the Hausfrau at her task. The floors, the window-ledges, the frame of the doors, the windows, cleaned and polished and gleaming in the evening sunshine. The place smells fresh and I suppose I dare not say anything about them. They are paid to work and they work.

The real cause of my mental disturbance is the one o'clock news. Dimbleby from Berlin has reported on the imminent rescinding of the Non-Fraternisation order. I still bear in mind what I said in London and intend to stick to it. As soon as the order appears I am writing a full length letter to Brodie and ask him to submit same to the War office. I cannot help but feel scandalised when each day I receive reports and letters from the men informing me that the Nazis are not being removed and that many officials in the towns in which they are billeted are the same as heretofore and that they are continuing to victimise the non members of the Party. Are we such fools or are we blind and inefficient? I can see the whole house of cards collapse so quickly and feel sick at heart. Nearly six years of war and death on all sides and still no lessons learned. I would not mind so much if the D.P.s could enjoy special treatment. But imagine the troops treating the girls to food and drink whilst our D.P.s receive no benefit from the military and have to continue to live on German foods given with a grudging hand. I cannot bear the thought. I do not know what Brodie's reaction will be . . .

When the withdrawal orders were published and non-fraternisation was no longer enforced, I wrote to Rabbi Brodie, my Senior Chaplain in London, expressing my profound concern as to the possible consequences. I was convinced that fraternisation between soldiers and the civilian population would inevitably lead to a devastating increase in venereal disease and the exposure of ill-equipped soldiers to the insidious influence of an ideology which would undermine the very purpose for which we went to war.

The attraction of the *Fräulein* would not merely be physical and sexual, but would tend to convey to the sex-starved soldiery that the Germans were not as bad as they were painted, whereas they should be made aware that the whole German population were accessories to the horrors perpetrated by the Nazis. I urged Rabbi Brodie to convey the contents of my letter to the War Office and sent a copy to the Assistant Chaplain General at 21 Army Group. Perhaps I was naive or foolhardy in taking such action. The repercussions were almost immediate; I was called to the A.C.G. who severely reprimanded me for daring to question an order issued by the Commander in Chief. He refused to discuss the matter and ordered me to write forthwith to Brodie withdrawing everything I had previously written and submit a copy to him.

I had no alternative but to obey and duly wrote a second letter, sent a copy to the A.C.G., but destroyed the original, thereby satisfying my conscience that I had given full expression to my fears for the future. To my great disappointment, Brodie, as was his wont, took no action and nothing more was heard of my protest. But fate can play strange tricks. Some year or so after I had left the army on demobilisation, I saw a report in the national press of an address delivered by this same A.C.G. in a Garrison church in which he deplored the increase in venereal disease among the ranks of the soldiers. I was sorely tempted to write to him and say 'I told you so'. But what was the use – the damage had already been done.

There were times when conditions were such that I found it far from easy to write to my wife. One such occasion was 20 July:

> ... Two more letters have arrived from you and the reference to our son and his affection is pleasing. Please darling tell him that I shall write more often and that he can number them. I hope the numbers will not rise to too great a height as I prefer

to be home with him and talk to him instead. Yes, my love, I feel a horrible sense of tenderness this afternoon to that little fellow and I have to thank God that he is well and alive. I buried a little boy of seven months of age this afternoon. It was the most pitiful sight. He died yesterday. He was born in captivity in one of the camps and his natural physical state was inadequate to stand up against the strain of living. His mother stayed behind in the camp and did not attend the funeral but his aunt did and her wailing was heartrending. She brought some clothing for him too so that he should be dressed before being lowered into the grave and to do this we had to open the tiny coffin and there he lay. The poor little mite. This is the first time I have seen such a sight and may it be the last. Thank God he was young enough not to understand pain and the little face lay there in repose as though in sleep. But his body was emaciated and partly green.

You can realise all too well that I do not feel like writing happy things at this moment, but I think back on that sweet sleeping little fellow of ours and realise that he has not suffered and nor have we and I am grateful. His mind works furiously and at times even you wonder what he thinks but he is healthy and normal and alive and vital and I am glad of it. I am longing to hold him tight ... and you ... and to whisper sweet things into his ear. Especially after a bath when he smells fresh and clean and rosy and his face gleams and his hair is combed and he looks angelic in innocence.

15

The problems of Belsen and the Displaced Persons prevented me from devoting due attention to my purely military duties. I therefore issued a New Year message, realising that the men would appreciate my situation and would join me in looking forward to the services to be held in the ensuing New Year.

TO ALL JEWISH OFFICERS AND OTHER RANKS WITH THE B.L.A.

With the passing of the Jewish calendar year 5705 and the arrival of the dawn of 5706 I take this opportunity of conveying to you and through you to your families my own and my colleagues' greetings and good wishes.

The last year of the war in Europe has ended. Our hearts are filled with unexpressed prayers of gratitude that we have survived the ordeal and that our families are safe at last from the terrors of the nights and anxieties of the long and difficult days. Soon we shall meet in various centres for public worship and shall take the opportunity of giving due utterance to all the deep-felt thanks which we owe to Almighty God for the benefits which we have lived to enjoy.

Many and varied will be our emotions during these coming High Festivals. For many of us it will be the last occasion on which we shall assemble at such services as members of H.M.

Forces. We shall inevitably recall the places where we have met
throughout these six years and the friends and comrades who
once accompanied us but who are no longer with us. We shall
recall to memory the many sacrifices upon the fields of honour
made by our comrades in order that the world might be
rendered safe for the generations to come. We shall remember
those countless sacrifices of civilians both at home and abroad,
of the millions of the House of Israel in Central and Eastern
Europe all of whom fell prey to the mad fury of the enemy. We
shall recall and not forget. We dare not forget for they have paid
the price for our safety and for the security of the world. We
shall bear in mind what this war has meant to our own dear
ones at home who have borne the pain and anxiety of waiting
for our safe return and have prayed that we might survive to
rebuild the desolated homes which once we enjoyed. We shall
recall all this and more and say in the language of the Liturgy
'We give thanks unto Thee for our lives which are committed
unto Thy hand and for Thy miracles which are daily with us.'
We shall meet in worship but it will be the time to think deeply
and subjectively. We shall escape for a day or two and
contemplate upon our own life and the meaning it has for us.

Where do we stand in relation to the world and its problems?
These Yamim Noraim are literally awe-inspiring days. Who
cannot help feeling moved when he places himself as the object
of self-analysis? It is the period of repentance. We shall examine
and probe ourselves and what can we contribute to a strained
and shattered world? What can we give in order that the lot of
others may be improved? Can we live selfishly?

The New Year dawns upon a world torn and broken. We
shall be faced with the problems which shall affect us as
individuals and as members of a greater society. We who have
suffered so much as a people have still much to contribute. The
world has still its lessons to learn and we have to serve as
teachers and guides, as understanding and enlightened men and
women. Perhaps even our suffering has left no impression on
others, maybe ears are deaf to the cry of the oppressed. Europe
is in chaos and its population harassed and miserable. The New
Year must reveal direction for us and for them. We have to
know where we stand and whither our steps are leading.

Soon we shall meet somewhere in this theatre, but not to rejoice. We shall congregate to indulge in communal thinking. I hope that your thoughts will be directed upon the lines I have indicated and that our mutual trust and confidence will strengthen us to new endeavours. We stood together in the line and in battle when our role was to destroy now we must stand together when called upon to rebuild. Side by side we stood and fought together with comrades of the House of Israel and other denominations. We must remain firm and loyal within the new ranks which are being formed for the greater and loftier task.

May you be given strength to carry on in this new struggle and may your efforts be crowned with the reward they deserve. God grant that this New Year may see the birth of a new and happier era for us and all mankind.

God bless you wherever you may be.

Yours sincerely

I. Levy S.C.F.

Senior Jewish Chaplain
21 Army Group, B.L.A.
August 1945

16

TOWARDS THE END of September I was recalled to London for a spell of temporary duty and was therefore prevented from participating in an historical occasion, a detailed report of which was conveyed to me by one of my chaplains. A two-day Jewish Displaced Persons congress was held in Belsen: a remarkable achievement due entirely to the efforts of the indefatigable Yossel, who not only succeeded in making it fully representative of D.P.s in the British and American Zones, but obtained the full permission of the military authorities for eminent visitors from abroad to attend. Among these were Professor Brodetsky, the President of the Board of Deputies, Mr Sydney Silverman, M.P., Mr Alex Easterman of the World Jewish Congress and a Mr Lurie, a war correspondent attached to the Jewish Brigade.

The tone of the Congress was set by Yossel who drew attention to the startling fact that within the last three months the number of Jews in Belsen had increased from 8,500 to 10,000 which imposed an additional burden on the Central Committee.

Serious attention had to be given regarding the future of all Jewish D.P.s in all the camps in Germany. They must be recognised as Jews not as Poles or any other nationality. Palestine was the only country that would give them the peace they yearned for and they would not relax their efforts to obtain recognition of this right to which they were entitled. Meanwhile Jewish centres should be provided which would offer facilities for self-preparation for a future in Palestine. (See Appendix C, p. 124.)

Hadassah Bimko, too, made a significant contribution to the deliberations. Her primary concern was the provision of adequate health services. Like other members of the Central Committee she was severely critical of the apparent apathy displayed by Jews abroad. The fact that German doctors and nurses were attending Jewish patients created an atmosphere of suspicion between the medical staff and the patients which was not conducive to their recovery. She urged the establishment of Jewish hospitals staffed only by Jews.

The general consensus of opinion was that Jews should be treated as a distinct and separate entity, that Jewish D.P. centres be established which would provide for their specific needs, and that priority be given to the ultimate solution i.e. facilitating emigration to Palestine. In drawing the Congress to a close the following resolutions were passed:

In the name of the six million Jews who have fallen victim of the German terror, and in the name of the survivors, we call on the peoples of the world and in particular the British people, who carry the responsibility in this respect, to recognise that the world will know no peace so long as the Jewish people is denied the right, which exists for all other peoples, to determine its destiny in its own land.

We call on the world to realise that the extermination of six million Jews in Auschwitz, Treblinka, Majdanek, Belsen and other centres was possible only because of the homelessness of the Jewish people. We demand the right to guard our children and coming generations against a repetition of this disaster. We shall appeal to the United Nations and to England in particular to end this homelessness.

We affirm our right of immigration into Palestine, sealed

with the blood of millions and demand its immediate realisation. We, representatives of the Remnant assembled here in Bergen-Belsen, express our sorrow and indignation that almost six months after the Liberation we still find ourselves in guarded camps on German soil soaked with the blood of our people.

We proclaim that we will not be driven back to the lands which have become graveyards of our people. We vow that no obstacle or political restriction will bar our way to Palestine and warn those concerned of the consequences which will flow from a political conflict with the vital interests of the Jewish people.

This Congress demands that as long as Jewish survivors remain in Germany they shall be recognised as Jews not as nationals of countries to which they do not intend to return. The Congress urges that opportunities be created for training the survivors for productive life in Palestine; that Jewish camps and centres be established both in the British and American Zones under Jewish administration and that Jewish liaison be appointed with the military government in Germany.

The Congress asks that the property of destroyed Jewish communities and of individual Jews who perished without successors shall be placed at the disposal of the representative body of the Jewish people for the purpose of further development of Palestine. The Congress asks that a special allocation be made from German reparations for life pensions for all Jews disabled and rendered invalids in German concentration camps.

This Congress requests Jewish representation at the International Commission for War Crimes. This Congress asks for the recognition of the Central Jewish Committee as the legal representative body of all former inmates of concentration camps in the British and American Zones.

This Congress states that five months after the liberation it is still impossible for the survivors to correspond with their relatives and demands an immediate change in this abnormal position.

The Congress greets the Jewish Brigade with which it feels itself united by ties of brotherhood and common struggle. This

Congress finally resolves that a memorandum setting forth the
conditions and the needs of the Jews in Germany, together with
the resolutions of Congress, be submitted to Generals
Montgomery and Eisenhower.

There is no doubt that this Congress reflected the determination of the Central Committee to improve the lot of the
inmates of the camps, the recognition of its own status in the
eyes of the military authorities, and the strength of its leadership. Unfortunately the passing of resolutions may satisfy those
who formulate them, but whether they produce the desired
effect is questionable. The Palestine question remained in
abeyance for some time, for the Mandatory authorities continued their policy for at least three years until the State of
Israel was declared. The creation of Jewish D.P. centres,
however, was under serious consideration and there was every
hope that they would materialise.

17

Shortly after the Congress, my spell of temporary duty in London came to an end and I returned to Germany to learn that before many weeks had passed I would receive my demobilisation orders. In the meantime a new administrative question arose, largely due to the initiative of the Board of Deputies and the Jewish Committee for Relief Abroad. As a result of representations by them to the Chief of Staff there was every possibility that an Advisory Officer on Jewish Affairs might be appointed to serve on his staff, and a list of names of recommended candidates for this appointment was about to be drawn up. I was asked whether I would agree to permit my name to be submitted as it was considered that I would be a most suitable candidate for such an office. Three days later, on 12 October, Leonard Cohen of the Jewish Committee for Relief Abroad wrote to me:

> I expect that you have heard from Professor Brodetsky that we had a meeting on Sept. 29th with the Chief of Staff, General Sir Brian Robertson and General Templar. I think that our proposals for Special Jewish Centres will at last be accepted. We are in a position now that we ought to have been in four months ago, and then when the decision is finally taken to

establish these centres, I am afraid we shall be well into the winter before the people are re-grouped.

Actually what I think to be one of the most valuable results of our representations is that General Robertson has agreed to appoint to his staff an Advisory Officer on Jewish Affairs. The importance and value of such an appointment will, of course, depend on the man appointed to the position.

I think I can express my own personal opinion and say that I hope that you will be the man appointed and that you will accept the appointment. I do not think I am betraying any confidence when I tell you that we are expecting to receive from the War Office within the next few days, a request for suggestions of names of suitable people. Apparently they do not want us to nominate one person, but to put forward several names. I understand that we are putting forward three names with yours as one of them. My own personal opinion again, is that yours will be the one which will be accepted by the War Office.

Actually at the meeting with General Robertson, I was indiscreet enough to ask him whether he would regard someone such as yourself as acceptable, and he replied that although he did not know you, it would be just someone in your position whom he would regard as most suitable.

I am writing all this because I hope that if the appointment is offered to you that you will accept, also that you will be prepared mentally for the appointment. I am myself building a great deal upon it for the work generally and for our own contribution to the work.

We have just made arrangements to come under UNRRA. Although the transfer from the Red Cross to UNRRA has not yet been completed, it will probably take place in the next two or three weeks.

Although UNRRA is to be responsible for running the Displaced Persons' Centres, I think a great measure of control will rest with the army and in particular a decision as to whether Jewish Relief Workers are to be sent to a particular place may still rest with the army. I feel sure that if you, as principle Advisory Officer, think that there is a need for workers in particular places, your advice would be taken.

We may be able to get our people in much more easily than we have hitherto; for instance, you have been to Berlin and have reported on the need for workers there. I was asked to go to Berlin but I decided it would be simply a waste of time to go and make another report as yours and Major Nadich's were available. What we needed were workers and supplies. I have actually asked for permission for Mrs. Henriques and Rabbi Munk to go to Berlin for a few weeks to make a full survey and to report on the needs. I had to do it this way because I was told that I could not ask for permission for them to go and stay there. In any case, of course, we did not want them to be there permanently. We should want to bring up three or four relief workers to assist the community.

I expect you heard all about the trouble with the Chief Rabbi's Council and Dr. Salaman. I think we are going to find a satisfactory solution to the problem. I will write and let you know the full details as soon as it is clear.

Flattered as I should have been by the terms of the suggestion, I could not help but reply in the negative to the Board of Deputies and on 19 October I explained my reasons for turning down the position to Leonard Cohen:

> ... I saw Brodetsky before and after his visit to Belsen and handed him a long memo on the matters he ought to raise at this H.Q. On his return he informed me that he had had a conversation with Generals Robertson and Templar.
> In my reply to the Deputies I stated that I could not accept the appointment were it offered to me or rather I could not allow my name to be put forward as I am about to be released from the army. The fact is that I am leaving here on the 24th inst. I also stated to the Deputies that I have grave fears about the new appointment in that an adviser may sound very fine on paper but what guarantee have we that good advice will be taken? I would prefer to see an Administrator of Jewish Affairs appointed who would have some staff appointment and administrative responsibility. Control Commission leaves much to be desired from all appearances at the moment.

I am faced with another problem which is far from easy to solve. I have been away from home for nearly 4½ years and the strain is beginning to tell on me and the family. I cannot disrupt the whole of my domestic life in this way. In addition, the claims of the community in London are growing. My infrequent visits to London constantly call forth the question 'when are you coming back?' The United Synagogue is about to declare its vacancies and I have been asked to return to civilian duties as soon as possible. I just do not see how I can sever my connection with the community back home. Were I to stay away for another year ... and the suggested appointment would involve at least that length of time ... I would have no place in the community on my ultimate return. I am faced with a dilemma as you can see. I think it would be best if you tried to find someone else who could approach the problem with an open mind.

The impasse with the Chief Rabbi's Council is all too well known to me. I have read that they have broken away from the J.C.R.A. That would prove no obstacle provided that the troublesome ones were removed from here. I have had two sittings with the Rabbis in Belsen recently and have convinced them of the need for close co-operation. The scheme to split the orthodox from the non-orthodox elements within the camp would be fatal.

May I conclude with one offer. Even though I may sever my physical connection with the work here within the next few days, I would like to be of assistance to you when back in the U.K. I am off for a short rest in November and then shall return, I hope, fit for action. If I can be of service to the J.C. R.A. and the Committee for Jews in Germany I am at your disposal.

Many thanks for all your help and co-operation during my period of office.

I was not surprised to learn that in spite of all the promises, no such appointment was made.

Now the time had come to bid farewell to all my friends in Belsen. I could only hope that whoever succeeded me as the Senior Jewish Chaplain to the British Army of the Rhine would not be called upon to suffer the anxieties and heartaches which had been my lot during the seven hectic months I had spent in and out of Belsen. My consolation was that by then the Jewish Relief Team was doing excellent work, had developed harmonious relations with the Central Committee, had established schools for the children, and a workshop for the adults. The Central Committee was recognised as the representative voice of the Jewish D.P.s and Yossel had come into his own.

A permanent Jewish memorial had been erected in the former death camp where the mass graves now bore markers stating how many bodies were buried in each of them.

All that was now required was a definite policy to be devised for the ultimate dispersal of the many thousands of Belsen's inmates. Alas, this would not be realised for some time.

POSTSCRIPT

I NEXT VISITED Belsen in 1953 when I was invited by the World Jewish Congress to participate in the ceremony of dedication of the international memorial which had been erected on the site of the former Camp No. 1, where the mass graves were located. The ceremony was due to take place on the Sunday morning and I therefore flew to Hamburg on the previous Friday as I would not travel on the Shabbat. I was met at the airport by a representative of the Jewish community whose survival was largely due to the fact that he had been severely wounded in the First World War, and to the intervention on his behalf by his non-Jewish wife.

Passing through the airport control I experienced what I can only describe as a resurgence of German post-war arrogance. The official asked me how much money I had brought into the country. I told him the amount was £5 – all that was then permitted to be taken out of England. '*Nicht viel*' (not much), he retorted, to which I angrily replied '*Zu viel*' (too much), and with that the conversation came to an abrupt end.

Hamburg was *en fête*. It was late November. Shops groaned with food, the streets were decorated with fairy lights in preparation for Christmas. An atmosphere of prosperity abounded. So different from the Hamburg I had visited on V.E. day when I held a victory service in one of the halls which had survived the bombing in an otherwise devastated city. I could not restrain myself and expressed my surprise to my host. 'It is indeed ironic,' I said to him, 'back in England we are still rationed and everything is in short supply, yet here all seems so luscious and plentiful.' To which he replied 'Yes, you see *we* lost the war.' The word 'we' stuck in my gullet. This German Jew had completely identified himself with Germany's apparent revival. It seemed unrealistic – verging on the incredible – especially at this moment when our thoughts were directed to the ghastly memories about to be recalled on the morrow.

On the Saturday night, the participants and visitors to the ceremony foregathered. All of us were warmly welcomed by Yossel Rosensaft who was in his element, giving the impression that this was his crowning achievement. Among those present were several German Jews who had managed to escape to England in good time and had returned to Germany to resume their former professional careers, which at the time struck me as incongruous. Even more surprising was the festive atmosphere which seemed to pervade. I had expected a more sombre atmosphere redolent of the solemn purpose for which we had met.

The international memorial is in the shape of a tall obelisk, a cenotaph of sorts, backed by an extended wall. On this are attached fourteen tablets each commemorating, in various languages, the horrors perpetrated in this former death camp. Of these inscriptions, one is in Hebrew and another in Yiddish. Nearby is the Jewish memorial bearing in Hebrew and English the inscription, 'Earth cover not their blood.'

The ceremony of dedication was most impressive. Prayers were recited by a Roman Catholic priest, a Lutheran minister and myself – a truly ecumenical service. This was followed by a stirring speech by President Theodor Heuss who devoted his remarks to the sense of guilt which every German must feel. This site, which had witnessed such unspeakable horrors, would serve as a painful reminder of a cruel and vicious regime. The presence of the President of the Republic added profound significance to the occasion. Dr Nahum Goldmann, the Head of the World Jewish Congress, who followed the President, spoke with equal eloquence. He foresaw a hopeful future when a regenerated Germany would compensate for the suffering inflicted on Jewry.

The impression left by both speakers was that Germany was truly repentant and would ever be mindful of the sins of the Nazi regime.

Unfortunately with the passing of time, the memories seem to have faded. The poisonous seeds sown by Hitler and his henchmen did not die but are beginning to sprout afresh producing the treacherous fruits of neo-Nazism. In spite of ample testimonies of eye-witnesses and survivors to the horrors perpetrated during the Nazi regime, the passing years have produced pseudo-historians who attempt to re-write history, to deny the existence of the concentration camps, and the crematoria and the millions of victims who suffered torment and death. This blatant disregard of the truth, the appearance of neo-Nazis in Germany, and the recrudescence of racism expressed in the most violent form in the guise of neo-Fascism in various parts of Europe, the USA and even in Britain, prompted me to call upon ex-service personnel who had witnessed the tragedy of Belsen to assume the responsibility to testify to the realities of the atrocities perpetrated by the Nazis and to denounce the lies of the revisionist 'historians'.

To this end, in 1985, which marked the fortieth anniversary of the liberation of Belsen, I wrote to all the national and local newspapers throughout Great Britain announcing that it was proposed to hold a reunion of all military personnel who had formed part of the British Liberation Army. They were invited to reply to me stating their names, addresses and the units in which they served. For reasons of security the venue of the function was not disclosed, but those who replied were duly informed that it would be held in the Hall of the Community Centre attached to the Hampstead Synagogue, which I had served as its minister in the post-war years.

The response exceeded my wildest expectations. Over 300 replies came from all parts of England, Scotland and Wales and represented men and women who had served in 75 combatant military units as well as in various medical services, the Red Cross, the nursing services, the Quaker Relief Team and the Jewish Relief Unit. The atmosphere generated by these now ageing veterans of the campaign in Germany was electric, particularly when the representatives of the various units were called to identify themselves. They had survived their ordeal and could now reminisce on their experiences.

But the overriding sentiment which gripped them all was the fact that they had seen Belsen. Some had been with the first units to enter the camp and could recall the ghastly sight that faced them, 'How can anyone say that it never happened. We were there and we saw it.' Joyful as was the reunion of these veterans, their pleasure was only a prelude to the purpose of the function. They realised that the underlying purpose of their get-together was to ensure that none of them could remain silent and refrain from testifying to their bitter experience.

The highlight of this great and moving event was the showing of the film taken by Sidney Bernstein (later Lord Bernstein) when he served with the Allied Psychological Warfare Division. He entered Belsen with his camera crew and recorded the horrors in all their stark reality. His purpose was to show the film to Germans in order to convince them of the bestial outcome of Nazi propaganda. Although the film was taken on the express instructions of the War Office, it was never shown, the War Office having decided this would be inadvisable in the immediate post-war period. In introducing the film for the very first time, Lord Bernstein aged 84, emotionally described the effect that making the film had on him and his crew. The fact that he had been forced to keep it under wraps for 40 years added to his pain.

The film gave an added impetus to those former service personnel to increase the volume of their eye-witness testimony to the Belsen atrocities. As the reunion came to an end, I was convinced that the function had served its purpose.

It is, however, a sad fact that it takes far too long for the truth to percolate and the passing years will, alas, witness the diminution in the numbers of those who can testify from personal experience. Equally sad is the fact that it was not until 1993 that Lord Bernstein's film was shown on BBC Television under the title of *A Painful Reminder.*

APPENDIX A

Memorandum Submitted by the Welfare Department of the Jewish Brigade

6 August, 1945

The special interest manifested by the Jewish Brigade in the problem of the D.P.s stems not only from a humanitarian impulse to give succour to the most unfortunate victims of the Nazi regime. The Jews in the D.P. camps are our brethren not only in the broad connotation of the term as being members of the same nation and creed, but in the true sense – actual kin. Thousands of close relatives of this formation's soldiers are in the camps, and it was inquiries for the whereabouts of these relatives which brought officers and men of the Brigade to the camps, made them cognisant of the peculiar status and condition of the Jews there, and inspired these suggestions and recommendations for the amelioration of their lot and their ultimate rehabilitation.

I. *The problem of the displaced Jews* is a unique one. The victorious sweep of the Allied armies liberated millions of labour slaves collected from all corners of Europe and tens of thousands of prisoners incarcerated in numerous concentration camps. The Allies, likewise, overtook hundreds of thousands of non-Germans living in Germany for various reasons. The repatriation of these categories of non-Germans presented the victors with complicated political, economic and administrative problems. Enormous and involved as the general problem may be, that of the Jews is infinitely more so. They have been the most serious victims, subject to the most horrible tortures and indignities and what is far worse – extermination.

Those who have survived are scattered over the face of the globe. The overwhelming majority cannot and will not return to their country of origin which to them is no longer home, but profane ground fouled by the horrors perpetrated there, where even now hatred of the Jew is as rampant as ever. Life for the Jews in D.P. camps is not of the normal transitory nature but will be of longer duration where an atmosphere of physical and spiritual convalescence must be created. Special consideration must be given to their rehabilitation in accordance with their specific needs.

II. *The growth of anti-Semitism.* The problem has become even more complicated owing to the marked rise in anti-Semitic feeling among the troops and even among responsible officers. The reasons for this are:

1. Because of attempts to compel Jews to return to their countries of origin, many Jews fled from the camps and sought the protection of the nearby woods or villages. Having no other alternative many had to resort to living on the countryside for their subsistence, committing acts which brought them into bad grace with the authorities.

2. In many camps Jews are still placed in the same category as enemy displaced persons. The demands made by them for more considerate treatment irritate the officials who are reluctant to depart from their routine.

3. It is a regrettable fact that years spent in concentration camps have stamped their odious imprint on the character of the inmates with the result that ugly unsocial habits have become almost second nature. Many survivors owe their lives only to cunning and duplicity and view all acts essential for their well-being as permissible. Nazi brutality undermined their moral dignity and in their desire for self-preservation they cultivated low instincts and coarse behaviour. The superficial observer tends to compare the polite, courteous and humble German in defeat with the Jewish survivor and his constant demands for consideration.

4. The social contact between the military and the German population, which existed even before the non-fraternisation order was officially relaxed, was a factor in the growth of anti-Semitic feeling. The blonde German Fräulein is a better propagandist than the beaten, ragged and despondent Jew. Nor does this social contact between the military and German civilians, whose elegance may well have resulted from seized Jewish property, tend to assuage the bitterness which the Jewish survivor feels.

5. The uniqueness of the Jewish problem has caused great irritation to officialdom. Whereas all other nationals are relatively easy to repatriate, the Jew remains intransigent. This does not contribute to a kindly attitude.

III. *Special Jewish D.P. camps should be established.*

1. Those who were persecuted because they were Jews have the right to live as Jews. The continued evasion of recognition of the Jew's distinct national identity is in stark contradiction to their tragic reality.

2. Life under the Nazi regime has not tended to inspire any love for the Jew among non-Jewish nationals. On the contrary, intolerance and anti-Semitism has been well cultivated by Nazi propaganda.

3. The classification of Jews according to country of origin has led to their being billeted with hirelings and accomplices of the Nazis with ominous and disastrous consequences. In many camps a considerable number of non-Jews exercised their option of not returning home. It is not difficult to understand their motives. The majority of them were former Nazi sympathisers who joined up with the retreating German armies or were escaped members of staff of the concentration camps who had assumed false identities. For the Jew to live in close proximity with such types can only create bitterness and unease.

4. The frustration felt by Jewish inmates is not mitigated by the fact that a number of Camp Commandants admit the incongruity of the situation or by their admission of helplessness to alter this state of affairs due to the ruling imposed upon them. Many incidents have occurred where Jews have suffered insults and assaults at the hands of their so called 'Compatriots'.

5. The physical recovery and spiritual regeneration of the Jews can only be tackled when they are housed in segregated camps.

IV. *Pressure on Jews to return to their country of origin should not be applied.* Officials of various Governments engaged in repatriation duties in the camps, presumably working under instructions from their Governments, are doing everything possible to induce survivors to return to their country of origin whether for the purpose of solving the problem of shortage of manpower or for political reasons. In their approach to the inmates they stress that this is the last opportunity they have to return to their former countries or of communicating with surviving relatives or of ascertaining if any still exist. They convey the impression that those who refuse to return will be left behind with no one to protect them and would subsequently be treated as enemy aliens. As a result many survivors crazed with anxiety for the fate of their families from whom they were brutally separated, agree to return unaware of the consequences.

The following incident typifies the sorry plight of the returnees:
A transport of hundreds of Jews, in response to the overtures made to them, returned 'home'. At the frontier they were met by Government officials who informed them that they had all been sentenced to death for collaborating with the enemy, but as the war had been won, the Government had graciously commuted their sentence to three years forced labour to make amends for their crimes. The men were forcibly separated from their wives and children, loaded into trucks and sent away. A few escaped by jumping into the river near the frontier, others were shot and drowned. Those who succeeded in escaping returned to the camp to warn their brethren to avoid a similar fate.

Although we were assured that an order had been issued that there would be no compulsion to return to countries of origin, we learned, during a visit to Bavaria, that incidents had occurred when Jews who refused to return to their former country (Lithuania) were forcibly loaded on to trucks to be repatriated. Half of them succeeded in jumping off the trucks to take refuge in German farms and forests, the rest were taken away.

V. *Jewish survivors should be classified as Allied refugees and treated accordingly.* They must not be placed in the same category as enemy displaced persons who came from Germany, Austria, Hungary or Romania.

VI. *Camps should be open to receive the thousands of Jews who still wander about Germany and those who may come from the Russian zone of occupation.* Jewish survivors from Eastern Europe will trek from Poland, Hungary, Romania and Czechoslovakia to the American and British Zones either because of continued anti-Semitism there or because of their inability to strike root again in these countries. Whilst it is envisaged that the British and the Americans will not encourage such migrations, they cannot evade the responsibility of attempting to deal with these migrants positively.

VII. *Cultural, educational and recreational facilities should be provided and farms and workshops should be placed at their disposal for vocational training.*

VIII. *Teams of men now serving in the Jewish Brigade should be sent to the camps in the capacity of teachers, instructors and organisers of cultural, educational and vocational activities.* It is now unquestionably clear that only teams from our Brigade, men who speak the same language, sympathise with and love the survivors who are their own kin, who appreciate and comprehend their complicated situation, can provide the proper approach to these survivors, cultivate and bring about their spiritual convalescence and explain their problems and needs to whatever authority is in charge.

IX. *Authoritative Jewish communal bodies, such as the Jewish Agency, should visit the camps to clarify the desires and possibilities of the survivors as regards immigration and ultimate resettlement.* One needs to visit these camps oneself to see the men, listen to their experiences in order to comprehend fully the acuteness of their problems. Even one swift glance into the enormous chasm of their suffering will render a man unhappy for the remainder of his life and he will not find rest nor peace of mind until everything possible is done to atone for the indescribable evil done to them. One feels that this is not only one's duty as a blood relation, but a divine obligation imposed on all mankind irrespective of creed. That those now responsible for the fate of the survivors do not feel this need is a sorry reflection on the conscience of the victors. Although outside the massive gates of former concentration camps no longer stand the murderous Nazis with their bloodhounds, but standard-bearers of the civilised world, the road to salvation is still blocked.

X. *The ultimate solution.* It is clear that the segregation of Jews in D.P. camps and the amelioration of their lot are only temporary palliatives and provide no ultimate solution. Most of the Jews do not wish to and cannot rebuild their life in their former countries of origin. Entire communities seemingly deeply rooted, ended their existence in the crematoria and gas chambers of Auschwitz, Majdanek and Treblinka and the blood of their slain wives, children, parents, brothers and sisters is still before their eyes, and the sight of the bodies of their loved ones in the mass graves is still too vivid. Likewise the prevailing political, economic and social unrest in the Eastern European countries and the hostile attitude of their inhabitants provide little encouragement. Jews will migrate. Will the answer to this migration be only more D.P. camps?

There is only one ultimate solution. The White Paper of 1939 which condemned hundreds of thousands of Jews to destruction is now condemning the relative few who have survived to a continued rootless existence in D.P. camps. It was that same White Paper which both Churchill and members of the present government so strenuously opposed, as they did all other appeasement policies of the Chamberlain government, which must be repealed and the gates of Palestine opened wide to the hundreds of thousands whose only hope for a rebuilt dignified existence lies in that direction. Surely the policy towards the Jews should be based on principles of equity and justice and not upon falsely construed exigencies of power politics. The Jews who have given millions of victims to the Nazi machine and who have contributed over a million soldiers for its destruction, should be allowed that which even the nations which have spilt Allied blood were not deprived of – they should be enabled to create a national home.

APPENDIX B

Memorandum Submitted to the Chaplain's Department

June 1945

SUBJECT – GERMANY AND THE FUTURE

Introduction

Much has been said and written about the activities of the Nazis, their internal policy and their threat to the outside world. Opinions vary considerably as to the attitude which should be adopted by members of H.M. Forces to the individual German national during the period of hostilities and the subsequent occupation. These opinions range from complete nihilism to gentle understanding and sympathy. How often does one hear the opinion expressed that one cannot blame the poor simple German for the atrocities committed by the Nazi party.

The purpose of this paper is not to add to the already plentiful literature published on the subject, but to express the opinion and reaction of a Jew serving in H.M. Forces. The opinion of one who, closely knit with his own people, has felt the pain and the suffering of innocent human beings since 1933 and who has seen the inside of concentration camps and who has lived and worked amongst the victims of the obnoxious Nazi ideology.

1933 and onwards. Little can be added to that which has already been written about the rise of Hitlerism. From 1933 until the outbreak of the war many democrats, socialists and conservatives alike pointed to the menace of the rise of Nazidom. Looking back over these tragic years of war every thinking person must admit that all that was said and written was not exaggerated. Mass extermination, torture and the suffering of human beings were considered by the tender hearted to be impossible. The view expressed was that 'activities which are too terrible to bear description are too horrible to be committed' with the result that those of us who cried out from the Valley of Tears were scoffed at and laughed out of court. For a short period many thousands of Englishmen were affected by this contagious disease and Fascism reared its ugly head in England itself. Again we were told that this was a passing phase and merely the temporary madness of a few individuals. Perhaps they were right, but this could not be said of the continent of Europe. We realise now that the threat was an actual one and the consequences are now being borne by millions of men, women and children. Hitlerism in all its ghastly inhumanity has swept through Europe leaving a trail of death, disease, famine and destruction. Was all this perpetrated by a Party consisting of some eight million Germans or can the blame be laid at the door of the eighty millions of Germany's population? In the light of calm reason it should be self-evident that Germany as a nation must be held responsible and not just a small minority. Every German is an accessory after the fact. Hitlerism came into being by popular vote and, therefore, that which has been perpetrated was by common consent.

Herrenvolk and Conquest. The proud boast of Germany is its claim to racial superiority and its excuse for the extermination of millions of innocents is that thereby they remove a pest which has infected the body politic of the Reich. Once Germany itself had been 'purged' the desire to dominate neighbouring states gripped the fanatical mind of the Party's leadership. The hordes of the modern Attila spread across Europe. These neighbouring states were unprepared and even were they prepared were too weak to withstand the avalanche. Thus Austria, Czechoslovakia, Poland, the Netherlands, Belgium and France were overrun and even England, except by Grace of God, might have fallen prey to the advancing forces. During this period what was the reaction of the ordinary people of Germany? Did they display any sympathy for their neighbours? Did they not exult in the power so newly acquired? Were they not enriched by the plunder which their soldiers brought back with them? Surely no clearer indication exists to prove the non-sensical plea for the innocence of the German population.

Internal Policy. Now at last facts are available of the treatment meted out to the enemies of the state. Unfortunately statistics will never be accurately compiled, but it is all too well known that the fires of the Holocaust kindled by Nazism have exterminated six millions of European Jewry. And what of the Catholics, the Social Democrats, the Quakers, the Freemasons, the Gypsies and the Protestants who dared to raise their voice in protest against the ruthless policy of mass extermination? Does one still need proof that this is no longer an exaggeration? Yet, strange as it may seem, some still refuse to believe and give as the excuse that this is mere propaganda. Perhaps we ourselves are to blame in that we have been trained not to accept everything we hear and read. Buchenwald and Dachau were names known to the interested reader of modern German history, but now we have the testimony of eye-witnesses of what was perpetrated in the death factories of Eastern and Central Europe.

Eye-witness Account. The world now hears of the notorious Belsen concentration camp. I worked for some time in this camp and am, therefore, in the position to describe what my eyes have seen and which will haunt me as long as I live. Sixty thousand human beings lay cooped up in a camp six miles long by two miles wide. Food was denied them, their bodies emaciated from prolonged hunger. Death stalked abroad cutting down these innocent people at the rate of hundreds per day. On the arrival of the liberating forces, tens of thousands of corpses lay awaiting burial. The barely living lay in close proximity with the dead, using corpses as pillows and mattresses.

The living had no strength to remove the dead from their huts. Typhus, T.B., dysentery and other diseases raged throughout the camp and all the wonders of medical science could not save all of them. Death came as a relief to these hungry bodies and his scythe was sharpened by the whippings and beating with which the Nazis disported themselves.

Upon entry into the camp, the victim's hair is shorn and he is clothed in a thin striped material and exposed to all weathers with no more protection than this thin clothing can provide. Soon hunger takes its toll, the body weakens, the various diseases play havoc for there is no natural resistance and the victim dies and his emaciated body is cast into one of the mass graves.

I talked to those people who still had a minimum of strength to communicate and from them learned at first hand what they had suffered. For the majority of them this camp at Belsen was not their first experience of a concentration camp. They had spent a year or more in Auschwitz and elsewhere but all agreed that Belsen was by far the worst. The gas chambers and the crematoria were kindly compared with the lingering suffering experienced here. What is one to say to a woman who relates how her child was snatched from her breast and ripped apart before her eyes? Or what can one say to a man whose wife, together with hundreds of other women, was cast alive into an open furnace? One wonders how human beings can maintain their sanity whilst undergoing such unbelievable torment. And what of the S.S. and their Commandant who stand in parade as their victims are driven into the concentration camp to the accompaniment of an orchestra? The Commandant stands at their head and to the rhythm of the music swings his thumb to the right and left – right means life, left is death. Yet this is but a fraction of the mental tortures which the victims have suffered and is an infinitesimal part of the horrors which have been perpetrated in the death camps. These are the victims whom I met and with whom I spoke and with whom I lived. What was their crime? What can be the crime of any man to deserve that such a verdict should be passed on him?

Within a stone's throw of Belsen are the villages of Bergen and Winsen. One is prompted to ask, 'How did the inhabitants of these villages react? Did they not hear the screams of the victims?' But they stayed and brought up their children in this atmosphere and did not move away. Was this due to their fear of the Gestapo or was it indifference on their part?

The Future. Against the background of these considerations our future behaviour must be orientated. The army of occupation must reveal that if they do not come as avengers, at least they desire to prove to Germans that the day of their domination and dream of world power has ended. They must be made to realise that they have a sense of guilt for a crime against humanity which is heinous. We do not and cannot claim revenge. An eye for an eye and a life for a life cannot be demanded for every German murderer of hundreds has himself only one life to offer.

If we have made mistakes in the past, the possibility of correction has now come. Our future conduct is to be regulated by the order of non-fraternisation. There can be no alternative in our attitude towards a guilty nation. The Englishman does not understand the meaning of cruelty, nor is he expected to learn, but he is expected to be a realist and fully to understand that his enemy made his appearance not only on fields of battle wearing the uniform of the Wehrmacht, the S.S. or the Volksturm, but indirectly the man, woman and child who were, and still are, civilians are also part of that vast organisation. The mind of Germany is poisoned. The youth of Germany is misdirected. The future offers a threat to world peace. Our soldiers have fought and died in order that this curse may be removed and the world of the future may find peace and security. If we show weakness now, at the time of Germany's downfall, and take no steps to lay secure foundations for future generations, then our brave soldiers will have died in vain and we will have gained nothing from our years of sacrifice.

APPENDIX C

Memorandum Submitted to Professor S. Brodetsky, the President of the Board of Deputies

September 1945

1. DISPLACED PERSONS

a) *Specific Problems of Jewish D.P.s*: Those not desiring to return to their countries of origin are anxious to be considered worthy of special consideration and to be centralised in Jewish camps. The over-riding fear is that the authorities might forget them or form a ghetto within Germany. The vast majority ask for emigration facilities to Palestine. Further they require facilities for re-orientation, such as assistance to learn trades and for the provision of industrial materials. Belsen, for example, has asked for tailors', cobblers' and carpentry tools and for accommodation for the opening of work shops. Sugges-tions made to D.P.s to engage in agriculture within Germany have met with resistance in that they refuse to fructify the soil of the enemy. Further demands are for cultural requirements since up till now all schools opened within the camps have been of a provisional nature and ill-equipped. Special consideration must urgently be given to the opening of postal services for D.P.s. Military censorship has forbidden service personnel to act as intermediaries in conveying civilian mail.

It is essential to expedite the listing of D.P.s in order to help in the reunification of families. The latest introduction of a card index by the Central Jewish Committee will bear no fruit for at least six to twelve months as the search teams are too small in number to gather the appropriate information within the British Zone. Stress must be laid on the importance of centralising Jewish camps within the Zone of Occupation in order:-

i. To put a stop to the wandering of D.P.s throughout the Zone.
ii. To accelerate the re-union of families.

b) *Administration*: Until now Military Government has been responsible for the administration of D.P. camps which has not proved entirely satisfactory. Much depends on the quality of its personnel, many of whom were previously Civil Affairs officers. The integration of Military Government with the newly formed Control Commission has somewhat added to the confusion of the issues involved.

It is regretable that personnel within Military Government have displayed a measure of disregard for the human tragedy of D.P.s and have viewed their presence as an unwelcome burden. Control Commission is new to Germany and has yet to prove its worth.

With effect from 1st October, UNRRA is due to take charge of all D.P camps. In a recent interview with Sir Raphael Cilento, Chief of UNRRA in the British Zone, I was informed that UNRRA is about to submit an ultimatum to the War Office to the effect that unless full charge is given to UNRRA and complete co-operation is extended, in relation to supplies and transport, UNRRA would resign its responsibilities. Furthermore, Sir Ralph added, in the event of his receiving satisfaction from the War Office, he is personally in favour of establishing special Jewish camps. He impressed me with his warm sympathy for the Jewish issues involved.

2. GERMAN JEWS. The total number of German Jews returning to their former places of residence is daily on the increase but the estimated numbers cannot be stated. In reply to my approach to H.Q. British Army of the Rhine, on this subject, I have been informed, in writing, that so long as German Jews remain in D.P. camps they will be treated as D.P.s, but on their departure and return to their cities, they will be treated as German civilians. The reason given is 'for their own benefit and in order not to arouse anti-Jewish feeling'. At the

moment these German Jews have to rely for their protection on their local Burgermeister and much depends on the individual in office.

It can be readily understood that the de-Nazification of Germany is far from complete and some former Nazis are still in office. The plight of German Jews, therefore, varies from town to town. No regulation has been issued centrally with regard to redress for former injuries or in respect of restoration of Jewish property. Other than the letter I have received no ruling has been issued regarding the status of Jews. It is suggested that Control Commission be asked to promulgate some ruling which will be applicable to the whole of the British Zone.

The British Zone being divided into three Corps districts, rulings are issued individually by the Corps both in relation to D.P.s generally and to Jews of German nationality. The administration needs to be tightened and it is suggested that Control Commission be given some instruction from London which would be binding upon the Zone as a whole.

Furthermore, it is suggested that the authorities be asked to appoint a Jewish officer to serve with the Control Commission headquarters who will advise on the administration of Jewish affairs. It should be stressed that this officer should carry the rank, at least, of Lt. Colonel or else he would have no influence and be over-ruled by the most insignificant of local officials.

APPENDIX D

Jews of Berlin

3 August 1945

ADDRESSED TO MAJOR W. R. HOLDSWORTH.
MILITARY GOVERNMENT, BERLIN.

I desire to place before you certain facts in relation to the conditions prevailing within the Jewish community of Berlin, and would request that these be brought to the attention of the appropriate authorities for their consideration and necessary action.

1. *General.* There are in all some 9,000 Jews within the city. These comprise:

a. Jews who have returned from the concentration camps, numbering 2,000

b. Jews who managed to survive by hiding from the Nazis, numbering 1,000

c. Jews who married non-Jewesses but were still forced to wear the yellow star, numbering 3,000

d. Jews who married non-Jewesses but adopted the Christian faith and whose children were reared as Christians and were exempted from wearing the yellow star, numbering 3,000.

2. *Opfer des Fascismus.* It is well known that those persons who enjoy

the title of 'Victims of Fascism' are now receiving extra rations, are placed in the category to receive Ration Card No. 1, receive assistance with clothing and are given special privileges in relation to housing. The qualification necessary to enjoy these advantages is calculated in association with the Socialist and Communist parties and only political considerations are taken into account. It is, however, known that Jews are not qualified to receive such privileges just because they are Jews in spite of their suffering under the Nazi regime. I am certain that the democratic world would be appalled were it to learn that the Jews, who were the first victims of the Nazis, are deprived of any privilege of suffering. I would ask that special consideration be given to this matter and that the higher authorities review the whole situation in the light of the irregularities prevailing in the recognition of Nazi victims, and that a special investigation be undertaken into the activities of that branch of the *Sozialamt* which issued the privileged passes and *Ausweis* for *Opfer des Fascismus*.

3. *Ration Cards.* I am informed that with effect from 1st August Jews are to receive an improvement in the issue of ration cards in that they will be given one card higher than that received till this date. It is, however, pointed out that this will not solve their special problem in that for many of them the present state of categorisation of card distribution is inadequate. Most of them still receive Card No. 4 (previously holders of No. 5) owing to the fact that their state of health prevents them from obtaining work of the heavier type. In all fairness it cannot be expected that those who suffered so much at the hands of the Nazis should be fit enough to be so employed. Special consideration should be given in their case and ways found whereby they should receive at least Card No. 1 together with all those who have been recognised as victims of the regime.

4. *Suggested Means of Distribution.* Within a few days a full register of Jewish inhabitants will be available at the offices of the Jewish Community, 28 Oranienburger Strasse. It is suggested that after due consideration has been given to the needs of the Jewish population, that the lists of Jews held at the Community be examined and allocation of ration cards be made in collaboration with these offices. In order to avoid any possible abuse, allocation be made on the basis of the nominal rolls of those categorised in para. 1 above. It is further

urged that the principle regarding qualification as *Opfer des Fascismus* be amended to include all those who have suffered for whatever reason, and not to accept the membership of a political party as the only qualification.

Following the dispatch of the above memorandum, I sent a report on the condition of the Jews of Berlin to the Board of Deputies in London. This contained a résumé of the facts as stated above but with the following additions:

Communal Organisation.
a) Kinderheim in Moltke Strasse houses 60 children. Many are not Jewish or are *Mischling*
b) Jewish hospital in Iranische Strasse is still functioning, though most of the patients are non-Jews. The staff of doctors and nurses are all Jewish.
c) Altesheim in Iranische Strasse, formerly used as a D.P. Transit Camp is now housing returnees from the camps.
d) Synagogues. Rykestrasse damaged by bombardment but likely to be repaired in time for Rosh Hashanah. Pestalozzi and Joachimsthaler are improvised places of worship using halls in the original *Gemeinde* building. Services are held in these three places every Friday and Saturday.

Central Organisation. Some doubts have been expressed as to the personnel running the central *Gemeinde*. No elections have been held. But work goes on and strenuous efforts are being made to register all the survivors in the city. A considerable sum of money belonging to the *Gemeinde* was frozen by the Nazis. Efforts are being made to have it restored to the present *Gemeinde*, but the prospects are not promising.

Immediate Requirements. The state of health of the surviving Jews is pathetic. All complain of hunger. They ask for food to be sent by the Joint and suggest that it come via Denmark. Clothing is urgently needed. The children in the Kinderheim are almost barefoot and dressed in what approximates to rags. They require Schechitah knives and urge that the religious organisations in London provide them, and also instruments for Brit Milah. The winter is looked to with dread. I fear that many will not survive unless help arrives soon.

Whilst in Berlin I approached the General commanding British troops and he has promised to raise the issue of the granting of a higher ration scale to those who have returned from the camps with the Kommandatura (Central High Command). He could not promise more and suggested that the matter be taken up in London.

APPENDIX E

Belsen Associations

Some years after Belsen camp was disbanded and its inmates departed from the blood-soaked soil of Germany to take up residence in various parts of the world, Yossel Rosensaft, then living in New York, created the World Federation of Bergen-Belsen Associations. Modelling himself on the principles established in Belsen embodied in the work of the Central Jewish Committee which he led with such distinction, he devoted himself to the World Federation, in order to ensure that former inmates remained in contact, perpetuated the brotherhood formed during the period of their incarceration and, where possible, instituted a form of mutual aid when circumstances so required.

In addition, Yossel sponsored the creation of a Remembrance Award for excellence and distinction in literature of the Holocaust. To this end he formed an International Jury composed of twenty distinguished literary figures whose task was to decide on the recipients of this prestigious prize.

In February 1969, a formal Remembrance Award conference was held in London, preceded by a celebratory dinner which was addressed by the Israeli Ambassador Aharon Remez, the President of the Board of Deputies, Yossel Rosensaft and the guest speaker, Elie Wiesel. The privilege of presiding at this function was accorded to me and I delivered the following opening remarks:

Twenty-four years have passed since the guns of World War II were silenced, since the fires of the crematoria were extinguished, since the gates of the hell camps were opened and the remnant of our people – a broken and scarred remnant – emerged to breathe the fresh air of freedom.

For some, these twenty-four years is a life time. A new generation has been born since then for whom the Holocaust is not a personal experience, but a chapter of past history. A chapter written either by those who knew it, lived it and suffered it, or just a chapter of human history which is already being variously depicted. Truthfully by some, but re-written by others in order to minimise the horror or to reduce the measure of the Jewish calamity. For us who lived through this period, who suffered it physically either by incarceration or deportation or by the measure of personal service we were privileged to render, it is a living memory, a bitter memory and an unforgettable experience. We may not bear the tattoo marks on our arms, but we carry with us the memory of the pain, the *Judenschmerz*, that this upheaval inflicted on us.

If I may speak very personally, let me confess here and now that I cannot recall Belsen without remembering my first entry into the camp a few days after its liberation. The scene which I witnessed then is as vivid now as it was then. I stood among the living and the dead, hardly distinguishing between the one and the other. In my mind's eye I still see the living, but barely living skeletons, and the mass graves at which I stood reciting the kaddish. I recall the anguish of those ill-fated inmates and their joy at the sight of a Magen David on a British uniform. I hear the Yiddish word and relive the embrace of welcome. The sound of young people speaking fluent and beautiful Hebrew still rings in my ears, and I can see on their faces the expression of yearning to be out and away *en route* for Eretz Yisrael.

I recall our tussles with the authorities to convince them that these men and women were Jews who wished to be known as such and not as Poles, Hungarians or other nationals and as Jews they wished to remain united and not transferred to camps where Poles and other nationals were being herded for ultimate repatriation. I remember, too, how we fought to obtain certificates for admission to Palestine and none were forthcoming.

These are only some of the recollections which flood in as I think back to those distant, and yet not so distant days.

This is a chapter of history which must not be erased from human memory. It was at Belsen that we took the oath never to allow the enormity of Jewish sacrifice to be forgotten. But how will the memory be perpetuated? When we are no longer here to tell the tale, who will pass the story on to future generations?

It is primarily for this reason that the Remembrance Award was created, so that literature shall enshrine the memory of the Holocaust, the Churban, that barbaric destruction of so much that was so fine in the Jewries that were inhumanly annihilated.

Today, eminent men of letters have deliberated on the written contribution to Churban literature, and although I do not yet know who will receive this year's award, of one thing I am certain, that encouragement will be given to add to the corpus of literature, thereby ensuring that those of our people, who were so mercilessly destroyed will have their sacrifice truly and faithfully recorded for the enlightenment of future generations. I deem it a great honour to have been invited by our dear friend, Yossel, to take the chair at this function. I dare not claim that I know the reason for this distinction. Perhaps it is because I was the first British Jewish Chaplain to meet him in Belsen and because we worked so closely together during those early hectic days and months. Whatever the reason, I am greatly honoured and humbly grateful to be privileged to open these proceedings.

APPENDIX F

Brigadier H. L. Glynn Hughes

Memories of Belsen never fade, but incidents occur which cause such memories to flood in with exceptional poignancy. Such an occasion was the memorial service held on 8 January 1974 to offer thanksgiving for the life of Brigadier Glynn Hughes who died the previous year aged 81. His experience of the horrors of Belsen moved him profoundly and left him with a deep attachment to the Jews who survived. His association with them continued long after his release from military duties and he maintained close contact with the Rosensafts and with many survivors. In his Will he left instructions that should any form of service be held in his memory a special prayer for the survivors of Belsen should be recited. He further added that were I available, he hoped that I would compose such a prayer and recite it.

I gladly complied with his wishes. I regarded it as a special privilege to participate in paying tribute to this remarkable man who not only rendered such life-saving service to so many thousands of Hitler's victims after their liberation, but maintained contact with many of the survivors, befriended them, visited many of them in Israel and showed concern for their welfare to the very end of his long life.

The service was held at the St Marylebone Parish Church and was conducted by the Rt Rev Victor Pike, my former Assistant Chaplain General, now Bishop of Sherborne, with whom I crossed swords on several occasions but who, on this occasion greeted me as a long-lost brother. The following is the text of the prayer which I was privileged to compose and recite:

O God, mighty and revered, we come before thee this day to render thanks for thy mercies and to express submission to thy Will. We recall the pain and anguish suffered by so many tens of thousands who were ruthlessly incarcerated in such death camps as Bergen-Belsen. We mourn all those who died from hunger, disease and cruel torment and whose wasted bodies were interred in the mass graves of the camps. We call to mind the years of bitter suffering which they underwent under a merciless regime and pray that never again may men suffer the degradation of such dire inhumanity.

But as for those who survived the torment, we remember with gratitude and affection the brave men who entered the death camps to give succour and medical aid to the ailing, the weak, the starving and the tormented. Heedless of the risk to their own life and of exposure to the diseases rampant in the camp, they toiled ceaselessly to save the remnant of a tortured people. By Grace of God and by their labours many were snatched from the jaws of death and now live in freedom in the lands of their choice.

On their hearts are lovingly engraved the names of Hugh Llewelyn Glynn Hughes, his medical colleagues, and those officers and men of the Forces who, inspired by his selfless devotion, so faithfully tended the needs of suffering humanity. We unite with them in gratitude and share with them the hope and the prayer that they may end their days in peace and pass on to their children the recollections of the love and kindness and humaneness displayed to them so that in the fullness of time men may learn to live together in amity, to unite in constructive living, to remove bitterness and enmity and so hasten the day when, in the words of the prophet, 'swords will be turned into ploughshares and spears into pruning hooks and men will not learn war any more'. 'When the world will be perfected under the Kingdom of Almighty God and all the children of flesh will call upon His name'.

I deemed it appropriate to send a copy of the Order of Service and this prayer to Yad Vashem in Jerusalem where all those who were honoured by the title 'Righteous Gentiles' are recorded. Brigadier Glynn Hughes would certainly be worthy of inclusion among those who helped to save Jews from Nazi torment.

In acknowledging my communication the Director of Yad Vashem wrote:-

The Order of Service held in honour of the late Brigadier Glynn Hughes including the prayer for the survivors of Bergen-Belsen, recited in accordance with the special wish of the late Brigadier, represents a remarkable document proving that there need not be barriers between the faiths and that men can love, respect and help each other, not withstanding differences of religion.